Return to Philosophy

AMS PRESS

NEW YORK

Return to Philosophy

being

A Defence of Reason
An Affirmation of Values
and A Plea for Philosophy

by

C.E.M. Joad

NEW YORK

E. P. DUTTON & CO., INC.

Library of Congress Cataloging in Publication Data

Joad, Cyril Edwin Mitchinson, 1891-1953.
    Return to philosophy.

    Reprint of the 1936 ed. published by E.P. Dutton,
New York.
    Includes index.
    1. Philosophy. 2. Reason. 3. Truth. 4. Worth.
5. Huxley, Aldous Leonard, 1894-1963. I. Title.
B1646.J73R4 1976   192   75-41157
ISBN 0-404-14559-0

Reprinted from an original in the collections of
the University of Iowa Library
From the edition of 1936, New York
First AMS edition published in 1976

Manufactured in the United States of America

AMS PRESS INC.
NEW YORK, N.Y.

Foreword

★

Many people to-day adopt an instinctively derogatory attitude to reason. It is not, they say, a free activity of the mind, reaching conclusions under no compulsion save that of the evidence; it is the tool of instinct and the handmaid of desire. They are sceptical also in their attitude towards values. Beauty, they hold, is not an intrinsic quality of things; it is merely the compliment which we bestow upon the objects which have been fortunate enough to give us pleasure. One man's pleasure is as good as another's, and all the art criticism in the world is only an elaborate series of variations upon the theme: 'This is what I happen to like.' As with art, so with morals. To act rightly is merely to act in a way of which other people approve.

It is the object of the following pages to criticize this subjectivist attitude and to expose its inadequacy in art, in morals, and in thought. The book is, therefore, in effect a restatement in modern terms of certain traditional beliefs; that reason, if properly employed, can give us truth; that beauty is a real value which exists, and that we can train our minds and form our tastes to discern it; that some things are *really* right in a sense in which others are *really* wrong, and that the endeavour to know truth and to discern value is the noblest pursuit of the adult civilized intelligence. The best name for this pursuit is philosophy. This conclusion is reached by a number of different routes, each of which starting from some distinctive characteristic of modern life or thought, an aeroplane shed, a quasi-religious cult, or an essay of Aldous Huxley converges upon the same position. The defence of reason, the affirmation of values and the plea for philosophy thus constitute the underlying theme which links together the various essays which follow.

C.E.M. JOAD

Contents

★

CHAPTER		PAGE
	Foreword	7
I	'Bunkumismus' or Reason's Underworld	11
II	Defence of Value—I. Value in the Modern World	58
III	Defence of Value—II. Beauty	94
IV	Defence of Value—III. Aldous Huxley and the Dowagers	113
V	Defence of Reason—I. Reason and Truth	139
VI	Defence of Reason—II. Reason and Conduct	175
VII	Defence of Philosophy—I. Philosophy and Life	201
VIII	Life into Value	216
IX	Defence of Philosophy—II. Philosophy and Value	246
	Epilogue	271
	Index	277

My thanks are due to the Editor of *Philosophy* for permission to reprint Chapter VII, which originally appeared in the *Journal of Philosophical Studies*.

Chapter I

'Bunkumismus'[1] or Reason's Underworld

★

'Measles, rheumatics, hooping-cough, fevers, agers, and lumbagers', said Mr. Squeers, 'is all philosophy together; that's what it is. The heavenly bodies is philosophy, and the earthly bodies is philosophy. If there's a screw loose in a heavenly body, that's philosophy; and if there's a screw loose in a earthly body, that's philosophy too; or it may be that sometimes there's a little metaphysics in it, but that's not often. Philosophy's the chap for me. If a parent asks a question in the classical, commercial, or mathematical line, says I, gravely, "Why, sir, in the first place, are you a philosopher?" "No, Mr. Squeers," he says, "I an't." "Then, sir," says I, "I am sorry for you, for I shan't be able to explain it." Naturally the parent goes away and wishes he was a philosopher, and, equally naturally, thinks I'm one.'—Mr. Squeers in *Nicholas Nickleby*.

i

Meals with the Great. I have frequently been surprised by the appeal of philosophy to successful men of the world. Those who have achieved wealth, eminence and power by virtue of being hard-headed practical men with no nonsense about them, seem late in life to de-

[1] With acknowledgements to W. J. Turner for coining the only possible word.

velop a kind of soft spot in the brain through which, mysteriously, philosophy creeps. Sooner or later, if I may mix my physiology, the hardest head develops its Achilles heel, and this Achilles heel is a conviction that its owner is an original metaphysician. As a professional philosopher who has written a number of philosophical books, it has been my lot to come into contact with a number of such men during their late metaphysical periods. The contact has usually begun with the arrival of a discreet note from some well-known man of affairs, asking me to lunch or dinner. Highly gratified and pleasantly expectant of some proposal redounding to my credit or profit, I have accepted.

I am surprised at the modesty, at the diffidence almost, with which the great man receives me, especially when it becomes clear that a *tête-à-tête* between myself and my host is intended. During the meal, usually an admirable one, we talk on indifferent topics; he volubly and assertively, I gradually subsiding into the muddled acquiescence which good wine causes me to extend to all opinions, however outrageous. Yet behind the volubility and the assertiveness, the diffidence, it is obvious, is still there. By the time the table has been cleared, coffee served, cigars lighted, decanters placed on the board and the servants withdrawn, it has become unmistakable nervousness. A sort of imminence gradually creeps into the atmosphere; a disclosure, it is clear, is impending.

After-Dinner Philosophy. The Universe Unriddled. And

presently out it comes. My host, it seems, has for years past been giving his attention to philosophical subjects. He has, he knows, no training in philosophy, but he has been interested in it all his life. As a token of this lifelong interest he has drawn up a scheme, a plan, a system, theory or formula, the fruit of prolonged meditation, which he believes to be not entirely without importance. Growing enthusiastic as he proceeds, he divulges that the scheme, plan, system or what not, is nothing less than a complete philosophy of the universe, in the course of which all problems which have at various times puzzled philosophers are finally set at rest.

This scheme he has resolved to lay before me, and with an exquisite mixture of diffidence and condescension he finally produces from a drawer a typewritten manuscript, carefully sealed and swathed in tape. The seal is elaborate, the tape brightly coloured, the typing exquisite. And that is all! As for the contents, the scheme, system, theory, philosophy, it has turned out with practically no exceptions to be complete balderdash, the degree of its sense being inversely proportional to the magnitude of its pretensions.

In this way I have been honoured in strict confidence with a private and advance view of the philosophies of a newspaper proprietor, a theatrical producer and the head of a big business syndicate, all men with well-known names at the very top of their professions, not to mention the meditations of smaller fry. And in every case the actual content of their solemnly divulged productions has been worthless. What they have had to say about life and the universe has been just nothing at all.

I cannot trust myself to reproduce actual conversations, but the following letter (whose authorship I must not for obvious reasons disclose), which, typical of a number that I have received following these intimate occasions, reproduces the atmosphere of faint reproach for my apparent unresponsiveness, my failure to be impressed, which they have usually sought to convey, will serve to illustrate the attitude and assurance of my eminent hosts.

'Dear Mr. Joad,

'I am sending you herewith a memorandum containing an outline of the scheme I had the honour of laying before you last night. It contains "My Philosophy", and after our talk I feel certain not only that you will be deeply moved by what you read, but that it will interest and enlighten you on many points which may previously have been obscure to you.

'I ought, perhaps, to say a word as to the origin of my thought. This is strictly supernatural. I believe that I have "recollected" (by the Socratic method of Recollection) a new meaning to the universe, and one which is not only compatible with scientific fact, but which throws new light on physics. I believe it to be the vision of the whole universe held by Socrates and, in a stilted and lesser way, by Spinoza. I began my philosophic studies with the Platonic Dialogues, and on the first reading "recollected", as it were, the real beliefs of Socrates. (I may have only recollected a justification for those views.) The Timaeus, I believe, because of Plato's reluctance to discuss the physical aspect of the universe, has not been given, during this century, the prominence that is due to it. I am convinced that this Dialogue contains information on the cosmical constant and its relation to the atom. At least I had knowledge from the Timaeus of such things before reading anything at all on modern physics.

'I have read extensively since my "recollection", and with, I hope, an unbiased mind, but I have found nothing in the accepted interpretations of Plato, nor in any philosophic system from Thales to Hegel, nor in the main theories of Jeans, Eddington, Einstein and Planck (in so far as they are compatible with scientific fact) to cast any doubt on my "recollected" scheme of the universe.

'My philosophy deals more particularly with the Spiritual side of life. I did not mention to you last night that I have had two visions both of which occurred in daylight. This is, however, the case and the system I have "recollected" is largely based upon them. This system has taken me years of hard study to prepare, but I am glad to say that I have succeeded with it so well that it now contains the key to the cosmos.

'I do not believe that such a comprehensive scheme which solves so many difficulties has been put forward before, and although what I send you is only an outline, you will, I am sure, realize that it contains the solution of all the traditional problems of philosophy, evil, matter, the many in one, the nature of being, and causation.

All these fall into their place in my general scheme like the parts of a machine.

'You will, no doubt, wish to communicate with me again immediately you have read the enclosed, and you will find me ready and delighted to listen to your comments and to answer any questions that may yet remain.

'Yours expectantly.'

A Philosophic Connoisseur. A short time ago an eminent book collector asked me to dinner. The name of this man is known throughout the literary world. It is a name which stands for high business capacity, a keen understanding of men and affairs and an unequalled knowledge of the value of first editions. Its owner is also known for his fine culture, his courtesy, his old-fashioned and liberal hospitality. As the novelists would say, he knows and is known by everybody worth knowing. He is the friend of many of the leading literary men of our time, and his friendship is deservedly valued.

I accepted the invitation. There were no other guests; the meal was admirable; so, for the first half of it was my host, whose conversation, which was full of anecdotes of famous people, interspersed with shrewd and amusing comments on the contemporary scene, gave me very great pleasure. He could explain exactly why Shaw's broadcast address in America was not a success, estimate to a pound the value of Hardy's various MSS., and appraise with a wealth of illustrative detail Arnold Bennett's vaunted competence as a business man. On these and kindred subjects, which were inevitably of great interest to an author, his comments were intriguing, his judgment shrewd, his knowledge prodigious.

About halfway through dinner, however, certain of the well-known symptoms began to appear. Slyly the mind of my host began to nod at me; intellectually he winked; spiritually he dug me in the ribs. There was a secretiveness, a hesitation which ill concealed the sense of a coming revelation. The significance which crept into the conversation was almost conspiratorial. . . . My worst expectations were quickly realized. Mr. X had, it seemed, been devoting his attention for some time past to what he called the cosmos. He had given to the subject the most prolonged meditation, often apparently to the exclusion of his business preoccupations. The preliminary fruits of these meditations he had ventured to commit to paper, and he was anxious to have my opinion upon them. It was his intention, at a later date, to set out his conclusions in somewhat greater detail, and then to summon the leading intellects of our time to a dinner—Shaw, Wells, Chesterton, Inge, Alexander, Bertrand Russell, Jeans, and Eddington, were, I remember, mentioned—at which he proposed to read to them the contents of what he called his last will and testament to mankind, which was, so far as I can remember, entitled '*The Nature of Substantive Being*'. Meanwhile, he would be glad if I would look through the preliminary draft, which in fifteen typed pages contained the gist of his philosophy of the Cosmos, 'the kernel', as he called it, of truth. He must, he had the grace to add, excuse himself for springing the thing upon me like this, but when I had read, I would, he assured me, understand his motive for acting as he had done, and he went on to imply—although the actual implication was left undrawn—that the importance of the subject matter would be found to justify *any* method of bringing it to my notice. And with an expression of absolute confidence in the importance of its contents and a hope that I should not be disturbed or thrown off my mental balance by the original, the shatteringly original import of its revelation, he thrust into my hand the inevitable roll of neatly ribboned manuscript, charging me to look at it there and then. With the eyes of my host upon me I opened, read, and was dismayed. The stuff was just pretentious balderdash!

Predicament of a Guest. Conceive the difficulty of my position. My host was, I repeat, a man of exquisite manners and refined courtesy. He had just given me an admirable dinner, thoughtfully chosen, perfectly cooked. I was at that moment drinking his excellent port, and now in a moment of confidence he was revealing to me the secrets of his private thought; he was making me free of his carefully garnered wisdom. I held in my hands 'his last will and testament to mankind'. And frankly I thought it nonsense. Three-quarters of it I could not understand at all; it seemed to me to be meaningless. The remaining quarter was a farrago of stale platitude and ethico-religious uplift. I am not usually unready in words, but on this occasion I simply did not know what to say. I could not even meet my host's eyes.

'The Rational Non-Mystical Cosmos'

He presses me to discuss arrangements for the dinner to Shaw, Inge, Alexander and the rest. Who should be invited? When should it be held? I shuffle and evade, for I know that there will be no dinner, and that, even if by some miracle these eminent men were gathered together at the same table, they would not listen to this kind of nonsense for a moment. Urged to say what I think of the preliminary draft, I am driven to subterfuge. And so I lie that I am going away into the country for a short time; if the manuscript is sent to me there, I will read it with more care and attention than it is possible to bestow upon such a document in London and after such a dinner. Will he, then, send it to me? Meanwhile I have had a delightful evening. . . . I make my excuses and depart.

In due course I return the MS. with a conventional note of polite praise. The habitual acuteness of Mr. X's knowledge of men and affairs must at this stage have supervened upon the naïveté with which he judged his own productions, for I was not again asked to comment upon '*The Nature of Substantive Being*', nor have I heard that the dinner to Inge, Shaw, Eddington and the rest has taken place.

'*The Rational Non-Mystical Cosmos*.' But although it may not be possible to induce thinkers to accept dinners, nothing can prevent them from receiving books. Even a person with as modest a reputation as my own receives yearly on an average some thirty free books about the Cosmos, the gifts of their authors.

'Bunkumismus' or Reason's Underworld

One such book which arrived this morning is before me as I write. It is called *The Rational Non-Mystical Cosmos*, by, as far as I can judge, an American business man. The book has been printed and published at the author's expense—my copy is called 'Third Private Edition'—and is introduced by the usual letter from an academic person commending the author for the brilliant originality of his work and drawing attention to its great importance. In this case the academic person is one Simeon J. Koshkin, who is an assistant professor in a School of Mechanical Engineering—not, one would have thought, the most suitable academic qualification for the giving of testimonials to universe-riddle-solvers. For it is as this and nothing less that Mr. Koshkin hails our author. His letter, which is headed '*A Dare to Science!*', after greeting him as 'Dear Mr. Gillette, Friend and Brother', proceeds to assure him that it is only men's 'serene complacence', their refusal to 'Think for Themselves' which makes them unwilling to admit that his book contains a solution of the 'Riddle of the Ages'. In spite, however, of this 'complacence', the book will 'provoke discussion and bewilderment', and if, because the author has 'Dared to be Original', he is overlooked in the present, he is comforted by the assurance that he can 'afford to calmly await the Verdict of Posterity'. . . . 'Mr. George Francis Gillette, you are in my sincere opinion an Original Thinker of the First Magnitude—and I dare anyone to dispute this!' So Mr. Koshkin in conclusion. . . .

And the book itself? Does it in fact provoke discussion

and bewilderment? Discussion, no! Bewilderment, yes! The Introduction invites us to an exploration in Mr. Gillette's company of the Cosmos. 'You are *in* it. You cannot ever get *out* of it. . . . Be a Cosmian. Not a mere Earthworm. The Gillette Unitary Theory is tendered as a Master Road Map of your entire property owned and run exclusively by Man. Or so he thinks.

'Look at It! See It All. . . .'

I have looked, I have seen and I can make nothing of it at all. There is a number of odd pictures; there are diagrams, scales, statistics, exhortations, continuing through 360 closely printed pages. But, as Mr. Gillette would and does say: 'Don't trust me, Reader! Look and see for yourself'; and, that you may the better do this, I had intended to reproduce here the first page of the text of his book. In fact the typescript of this chapter confidently announced that I *had* reproduced it. But, alas, while my MS. was with the publisher, *The Rational Non-Mystical Cosmos* has disappeared. I cannot understand this disappearance. *The Rational Non-Mystical Cosmos* is not the sort of book that anybody would wish to read, still less to steal. I tried myself to get rid of it by offering it to various purchasers both of review and second-hand books. All refused it. For weeks it remained prominently in company with other new books on a side table in my library. Then I took it and hid it away on an obscure shelf. From this shelf it has disappeared. Who, then, can have wanted the book sufficiently to have sought it out and removed it from its lurking place? And for what purpose? Somebody, it is obvious, has found some use for it. An enemy perhaps has taken it, or more probably, considering what it was, a friend. Or perhaps the mice. . . . But Mr. Gillette and his book are only an illustrative digression, from which I return to my philosopher hosts.

II

The Contrast. Looking back upon the incidents I have recorded, I am struck less by memories of my own embarrassment and the difficulties of extricating myself from my predicament without outraging the obligations either of politeness or of truth, than by the problem presented by the psychology of my hosts.

Here are men of proved business ability. Not only in enterprise and initiative, but in sagacity and judgment, they stand head and shoulders above the average of their fellows. In planning a deal, in driving a bargain, in sizing up a rival, in selecting an employee, in all these matters their success depends on the constant and efficient use of their critical faculties. Let them make a mistake in these matters, let them judge a man wrongly, erroneously estimate the probable results of a venture, employ bad servants, and their loss may run into hundreds of thousands. These, then, are men of critical judgment and acumen. Such men are difficult to impose upon. They are not the sort who are 'taken in'. They are not, for example, likely to mistake pretentious advertisement for solid worth. Nor in their own sphere do they. But directly they exchange the future of a theatrical venture for that of the Cosmos and begin to

22

speculate not upon stocks and shares but upon Being, their simplicity is as that of the most besotted revivalist, of the callowest undergraduate. Their clear-headedness is muddled; their acumen blunted; they are incapable of recognizing balderdash when it is their own, while their practical judgment does not prevent them from being taken in by whatever farrago of pretentious obscurities and cosmic flapdoodle may happen to have caught their ears.

Why Philosophy? It is further noticeable that it is not science that attracts these men; they do not study the classics; they have no penchant for mathematics or history; they do not even for the most part dabble in economics; it is to philosophy that they turn. The universe and nothing short of it contents them. The reason, I think, is not far to seek, and it is bound up with that modern belittlement of the intellect which is in part the theme of this book.

To acquit yourself creditably in science or mathematics, you need a keen and alert intelligence. You also need training and practice; you require, in fact, education in the subject. In philosophy the requirements are not different. But there *is* a difference and an important one. Lacking the qualifications you simply cannot do mathematics and science, and the fact that you cannot is immediately apparent.

In philosophy it is not so. The line that separates the profoundest metaphysical speculation from nonsense pure and simple is never easy to draw, and the latter may and often does masquerade as the former. It is this circumstance which constitutes one of the attractions of philosophy for the untrained mind. Even a fool can put up some philosophical show, and in no department of human intellectual activity is it harder to detect the fact that the performance is worthless. Hence philosophy is everybody's preserve.

While the main reason for the popularity and prosperity of philosophical idiots is the difficulty of distinguishing the fruits of profound speculation from the froth of undisciplined imagination, a number of subsidiary causes contributes to the same end.

(1) *Scope of Subject Matter*. There is, first, the all-embracing subject matter of philosophy. I shall return to the significance of this point in a later chapter,[1] where the practice of philosophizing is to be officially defended. For the present I am content to point out that, if the universe as a whole is the subject matter of one's study, it is extremely venturesome to assert that anything falls outside its scope. In fact there is a sense in which nothing *can* fall outside its scope. When one is concerned with the nature of being as such and the nature of knowing as such, it is exceedingly doubtful whether one is entitled to rule out any observation, however wild, as irrelevant. You cannot, therefore, when a fervent bibliophile draws your attention to the profound cosmic significance of the Egyptian pyramids, be *absolutely* certain that he is talking nonsense.

[1] See Chapter VII.

The Subjective Element in Philosophy

(2) *The Subjective Element in Philosophy*. In the second place, it is clear that one cannot in fact study everything. Therefore one selects, and selects according to principles which one uses as threads through the maze. How does one arrive at these principles? By reflecting upon what seems to one significant. Looking at the universe as a whole, one man marks evidence of beneficent creation and guidance, while another sees only a chaos of meaningless events. The general aspect which the universe comes, in the course of one's experience of living in it, to wear largely determines the principles which govern one's selection of phenomena for investigation.

Consider, for instance, the perfection of a fine summer evening. There is a sunset afterglow and an immense tranquillity predisposes the soul to reflect upon the beauty of nature and the beneficence of the creator whose handiwork it is. But not Thomas Hardy's. After an exquisitely moving description in one of his novels of just such a scene, he concludes with 'the cry of some small bird that was being done to death by an owl in an adjacent wood'. Of all the phenomena presented for his observation and enjoyment, this is the one which strikes Hardy as the most significant, pointing inescapably to the malignancy of the spirit that informs things, or to its absolute unminded callousness:

> '*Man's passions, virtues, vices, crimes obey resistingly*
> *The purposive, unmotived, dominant Thing*
> *Which sways, in brooding dark, their wayfaring.*'

It is a Thing which 'Works unconsciously. . . . Eternal artistries in Circumstance'.

Now the aspects of phenomena one selects as significant and the resultant principles upon which one's interpretation of the cosmos are framed, are, it is obvious, to a large extent subjective. This being so, it is clearly presumptuous to use any one interpretation as a stick with which to beat any other, difficult to say: 'It is perfectly obvious that you are talking palpable nonsense.' What I suppose one ought to say is: 'In the light of my philosophy it certainly seems as if you are talking palpable nonsense; but it is just possible that it is *only* in the light of my philosophy that it appears to be nonsense; from another standpoint it may not be nonsense at all.' And, if the views which I propose to criticize in later chapters are after all correct, if modern relativism can be accepted as final, if philosophies are, as Huxley avers, not only largely subjective but completely lacking in any element of objectivity, if his description of what we call thought—'men promote their fancies to the rank of universal Truths', and 'still imagine that they know something about the thing in itself'—is the beginning and end of the subject, so that one would be justified in saying with him, 'Science is no "truer" than common sense or lunacy', if, I say, these things are so, then it would be nonsensical to attempt a criticism of nonsense; for to say of a theory that it was nonsense would be a meaningless expression. It would be at worst a fairy story about the universe, projected into the external world by a mind that expressed itself in different fairy stories from those of the critic.

Huxley, who of all writers can bear fools the least gladly, is the least entitled to call any fool a fool. Still Huxley's view is sufficiently near the truth to make it more hazardous to dismiss a philosophical theory than a scientific one. It is unfortunate that his popularity as a writer should have made it more hazardous than it need have been. For it is, in part, to the widespread attack upon reason to-day, and to the general lowering of standards of thought and criticism which the belittling of reason has engendered, that the phenomenon of philosophizing financiers is due. Or rather, while the phenomenon no doubt existed in all ages, its prominence and audacity in print is peculiar to our own. Rich men with philosophical bees in their bonnets there must, I suppose, always have been; but it is only in Anglo-Saxon countries in the third and fourth decades of the twentieth century that they can count upon an audience for their buzzing.

(3) *Philosophy incapable of Verification*. Thirdly, there is the fact upon which I hope to enlarge[1] in a later chapter, that philosophical assertions are incapable of experimental verification. If a man proposes to make statements about the universe as a whole, he must, it is obvious, know the whole of the universe to be able to check his statements; if his conclusions purport to be true for all time, it will be necessary to have lived through all time to know that they are.

[1] See Chapter V, pages 172, 173.

'Bunkumismus' or Reason's Underworld

The following letter announcing the discovery of the truth about the universe which I recently received from a lady, will serve to illustrate my point.

'Dear Sir,

'I was deeply interested in your article in the ——. I think that in your turn you will be interested in my new Planetary Formation Theory which brings, quite naturally, in its train all that has been discovered: the solutions of present perplexities and hidden laws; while all phenomena of the Universe fit as closely as an epidermis. There is nothing in it that is inexplicable from the formation of the Earth up to the present, and its inevitable future is clearly pointed out. From this clarified view of Creation I have appended a short list of wrong conceptions, and am prepared to make this theory known to the world, when I can come in contact with a man of science who is willing to collaborate with me. May I suggest such collaboration for your consideration?

'Yours faithfully.'

Then follows the list of 'Wrong Conceptions', which is as follows:

'Theories of Creation; of Gravitation.
The Earth's centre as a molten mass.
The Sun as an orb of fire or heat; Sun-spots.
Planetary relationships; interstellar content.
Solar and Lunar radiation; Volcanic theory.
The finite and the infinite.

Eternity; the racial and the individual aspect.
God and the Demon.
Mind; cause of disease.
The what, how and why of being.
Life and Death.
Reappearance.'

To this list is appended the note: 'These are all rectified by the new theory of the universe.'

Now, in so far as the assertions included in this list are of a scientific character they are, I suppose, at least in theory capable of experimental verification. It is, for example, theoretically possible to verify the assertion that the Earth's centre is a molten mass, although the verification may be impracticable at the moment; while that the sun is 'an orb of fire or heat' was, I should have thought, not only theoretically verifiable but practically verified. But when we come to the more specifically philosophical items on the list, and consider examples of 'Wrong Conceptions' such as 'Mind; cause of disease' (presumably the 'wrong conception' is '*that* Mind is the cause of disease'), or 'The what, how and why of being', I do not see how it is possible to verify them. In so far as the alleged error of these Conceptions involves any assertion, it might be stated in the form: 'It is false to hold that mind is the cause of disease'; 'it is wrong to think that being has a what, how and why.' The only possible comment seems to be: 'Possibly, possibly not.' One knows of course that the statements are pure balderdash, the offspring of a brain badly attacked by the philosophical maggot; but I really do not see how one is to *prove* that they are balderdash.

Similarly, when somebody abruptly announces that the universe is ether, or that it is light, or that it is a mist of darkness surrounding a core of light, or that it is a 'structurated synthesis', it is impossible to be sure that there is no sense in which some one of these assertions might not be partially true. That matter is 'sensation in the sensationless', that it is 'life resulting in death and death in life'—announcements these by Mrs. Eddy—are assertions which to me are almost entirely meaningless; they are a mere putting together of words. But just because they are superficially meaningless, they can be shown by an ingenious commentator to bear any one of an enormous number of different meanings; and, in a universe of this size and complexity, one can never be quite certain that in some one of these meanings the words might not bear some relation to some kind of fact. It seems to me unlikely that they do; and if they do, the relation must, I should imagine, be incredibly remote. Nevertheless, one can never be quite sure that some grain of significance may not be hidden in this mountain of nonsense.

And the reason why one cannot is just this inability to verify by results, which is one of the great embarrassments of philosophy. It is an embarrassment whose appropriate consequence should be humility in assertion and tentativeness in conclusion. The measure of our uncertainty of truth should be the measure of our hesitation in asserting pretentious truth claims. Unfortunately the results have too often been precisely the contrary. Knowing that they cannot be called to the bar of evidence, men have supplied the place of knowledge by converting their conjectures into dogmas. In all ages they have announced *obiter dicta* upon the universe. But in none have they announced dicta of such overweening pretentiousness as in our own.

(4) *The Blessed Faculty of Intuition*. Fourthly, there is the blessed faculty of intuition. Intuition is a word which covers a multitude of intellectual sins. Of its employment as a method for the discovery of truth, and of the limitations of that employment I have written elsewhere.[1] I believe that intuition is one of the most valuable, as it is also the most lately evolved of human faculties, and that, rightly used, it is capable of exhibiting to the mind's awareness aspects of reality which are inaccessible to the logical reason. I believe, further, that this intuitive awareness of reality confers the most valuable experiences which the human mind, at its present level of evolutionary development, enjoys. The artist's appreciation of beauty, the love of the religious mystic for God, the activity of the mathematical or scientific mind in 'jumping' to the apprehension of new syntheses, are all in my view intuitional. Yet intuition is not, I would suggest, in the long run something set apart and divorced from reason. The truth of the matter seems to be rather that a chain of close reasoning carried out by a trained and disciplined intelligence prepares

[1] See my *Philosophical Aspects of Modern Science*, Chapter VII.

the mind for those cognitive 'jumps',[1] which are involved in the apprehension of all new truth and are the
appropriate culminations of all reasoning processes.
Yet these 'jumps', although they may be endorsed by
subsequent reasoning, are not themselves made by
reason in the strict sense of the word 'reason'.

But although a theoretical defence of intuition may be
made on these lines, it is not thus that intuition is normally employed. The resort to intuition is too often in
practice a device to avoid hard thinking, or a cover to
disguise the lack of thought. A woman's intuition about
people and things is the sort of thing that she has when
she is wrong; a philosopher's intuition about the universe leads him to announce conclusions which there is
no reason to think true. Those whose reason is trained
in dialectic will have little difficulty in finding plausible
arguments for any metaphysical belief they chose to
propound. Thus for their wildest announcements the
theologians and schoolmen could always invoke an
elaborate train of justificatory reasoning. To-day the
dialectical reason is as a general rule insufficiently
trained to be able to produce plausible arguments for
wild hypotheses and the bare pronouncements of the
intuitive faculty are usually held to be sufficient.

Public and Private Truths. The advantage of intuitive
pronouncements is that they need not be substantiated;
need not, because they cannot. In so far as a conviction
is communicable, it is reasonable; in so far as it is reason-

[1] See further Chapter III, pages 96-100 and Chapter VIII, pages
219-223 and 234.

able, it is communicable. This is not to say that there may not be convictions which cannot be supported by reason; still less that such convictions may not be true; but they must remain private. That seven times seven make forty-nine is a reasonable proposition of whose truth I am convinced. I can also undertake to convey my conviction by reasoned demonstration to anybody who is not an imbecile. I can make him feel what it is like to be convinced that seven times seven make forty-nine; I can make him see it for himself, as Socrates in the *Meno* makes the slave see propositions about triangles for himself. That I have a toothache is a non-reasonable proposition of which I am convinced; but, although I can make somebody else understand that I have it, I am totally unable to convey to him what having the tooth-ache is like, unless he too has at some time in the past had a similar experience. I cannot, in fact, make him feel my toothache for me, unless he has at some time or other felt it for himself.

Intuitive conclusions are in this respect like the tooth-ache; they remain meaningless to others, unless others have shared, in however limited a degree, the experiences upon which they are based.

Mystics and Others. Herein lies the root of men's difficulty in accepting the plain fact of mysticism. In so far as the mystic is one whose spiritual sensibilities are developed beyond those of his fellows, he is a biological 'sport' on the spiritual plane, and, as such, will enjoy experiences which are not shared by his fellows. And, be-

cause they are not shared, he will be completely unable
to describe or to communicate them. Language was invented to convey the meanings of this world; it cannot
be used as a vehicle for communicating those of another.
If, therefore, the mystic experiences the strictly unutter-
able, he will be wise to avoid trying to utter it. He does
try, nevertheless, and talks of 'a dazzling darkness' and
'a delicious desert', with the inevitable result that he is
regarded by the layman as an elevated madman.
Wrongly, since we have no reason to suppose that the
boundaries of reality are necessarily coterminous with
the intellectual horizon of the average twentieth-century
Nordic adult. The trouble is that the privileges of the
mystic in this matter can be and are claimed by non-
mystics, including the book collectors, financiers and
theatrical producers with whom this chapter began.
They too proclaim intuitive knowledge of the nature of
things, and, soaring on the wings of inspiration, look
down with contempt upon the pedestrian reasonings of
those who venture to criticize. There are matters, they
would have us believe, too high for reason. Or rather, as
one of them himself assured me, the heart has its reasons
of which the head knows nothing. How presumptuous,
then, of reason to intrude itself into spheres where it is
out of place, as when, for example, it presumes to subject to the processes of rational criticism a financier's
metaphysics. If they are inconsistent metaphysics, well,
then they are inconsistent. But how academic, how
pedestrian, how like a professional logic chopper to
point it out!

(5) *Influence of Psycho-Analysis.* For this current impatience with reasoned criticism countenance is found in current psycho-analytic theory. Freud and Jung and Adler, no less than Huxley and Lawrence, have combined to sow distrust of reason, and to represent it as a mere tool of the unconscious.

This doctrine has proved a godsend to fools. Those who are weak in the head have not hesitated to substitute the stirrings of the bowels for the processes of reason, and successful business men, equally devoid of a philosophical background and a critical training, do not scruple to present us with the truth about the universe in monographs of fifteen pages. Christian Science, Spiritualism and Theosophy, inner-light mysticism and the philosophizings of the Stock Exchange are the children begotten by intuition out of ignorance. They are perennial products of the human mind, appearing in a new guise in every age. Previous ages have contrived with more or less success to ignore them, with the result that sooner or later they have perished from inanition. But to-day psycho-analysis has come forward as a wet nurse to nourish and to foster, with the result that the nonsense mortality-rate was never so low and our age teems with the discoveries of short cuts to truth.

(6) *Difficulty of Determining the Philosopher's Credentials.* It is extremely difficult to say what the qualifications of a philosopher should be. If a chemist does not know the number, the order and the atomic weight of the ele-

ments, if a mathematician does not know his factors, if a geologist cannot distinguish primary from tertiary rocks, we recognize his incompetence and dismiss him as a fraud. If a painter cannot draw straight or an architect build straight, the fact is immediately apparent; but, if a would-be philosopher cannot think straight, the fact is not so easy to detect. Moreover, if he has the gift of words and has the good fortune, which he rarely lacks, to attract a following of those who mistake eloquence for argument and believe that, if a thing is said often enough and with an ever-increasing degree of emphasis, it somehow becomes true, he may never be exposed at all. Philosophizing is like acting and organizing in the sense that there are no specific marks or badges which can be produced for inspection as an assurance of their holder's ability to do his job. Philosophy, in fact, has no characteristic stigmata of competence. Hence, just as nearly everybody thinks he can act, and most people believe themselves to be organizers, so everybody can cherish the view that at bottom he is a bit of a philosopher with a reasonable measure of assurance that his pretensions in this direction, if he makes them known, will not be exposed.

But, when all is said that can be said touching the difficulty of discovering philosophical truth, the difficulty, when you have discovered it, of being sure that you have, and the difficulty of communicating your conclusions to anybody else, there are, it seems to me, certain qualifications which those who claim to enquire by the exercise of reason into the nature of things must possess, in the absence of which their speculations may usually be dismissed as worthless.

III

Qualifications of the Philosopher. (i) *Knowledge of the Thought of the Past.* First, he must have a knowledge of the past of philosophical speculation. It may be true that previous philosophers have spent most of their time in criticizing one another's philosophies, and that the corpus of philosophical knowledge which may be regarded as established beyond cavil is very small. Nevertheless, some conclusions may be taken as established, and it is desirable to know what they are, in order not to waste time in re-establishing them. Many mistakes have also been made; it is even more desirable to know what they are, in order not to make them over again. Moreover, some acquaintance with the critical methods of great thinkers engenders a critical attitude to one's own thought.

Even if it can be shown that the conclusions of the great philosophers were usually wrong, they were sometimes right. Now it is more important to know where a philosophy is right, than to know where it is wrong. Finally, whether right or wrong, all the great philosophers managed in the course of developing their thought to say a number of highly important things about human life and the way in which it should be lived. Even where the structure as a whole is unsound, the detailed work is often rich. Schopenhauer, for example, produced a philosophy which on its metaphysical side

37

is almost certainly wrong, and which, so far as its ethics are concerned, is revolting; yet in the course of its exposition he lets fall a number of detailed observations about things and people which seem to me to be of the highest value, and contrives by some miracle to establish a theory which is, taken in sum, the most appalling nonsense, by means of a number of separate observations which contain the most profound and original sense.

Schopenhauer's is not an isolated case. The treatment of special subjects by particular philosophers is often in the highest degree illuminating, nor is its value for us diminished by the fact of our disagreement with the philosophy as a whole. Butler's account of cool self-love,[1] and Aristotle's account of pleasure—to cite two instances which will crop up in the course of later chapters—are conspicuous examples of the power which the great philosophers have of extending and enriching our comprehension of life as a whole, enabling us to find in the world more challenge to our interest, more stimulus to our curiosity, more scope for our sympathy, our understanding, even for our passion, than we found before.

Thus it is not only for their truth or the lack of it, as I shall try in a final chapter to show, that we read the philosophers. To know what great men have said and thought in the past is one of the first duties of those who would think in the present, and those who claim to philosophize, neglect this duty at their peril. My

[1] See Chapter VI, pages 183-185.

financiers, book collectors, theatrical producers *et hoc genus omne* have completely neglected it.

Qualifications of the Philosopher. (*ii*) *Some Culture.* Secondly, it is necessary that he should possess some culture in the most general sense of the word. Culture may be partially defined as a concern with those matters which do not concern one personally and which cannot possibly conduce to one's advantage. To this extent my rich friends, owing to the circumstance of their having become preoccupied late in life with cosmic matters, may be regarded as cultured. I do them the justice to concede that it was not the desire to increase their wealth, to enhance their social reputations, or even— although this was no doubt a subsidiary motive—to achieve celebrity as thinkers, that prompted them to write their nonsense.

But the definition, although true so far as it goes, is not exhaustive. Some knowledge of the past achievements of the race and, more particularly, of its art and thought, some acquaintance with and respect for its traditions, some capacity not only for criticism but for appraisement of the work upon which its traditions are based, all these are essential parts of culture. Together they build up certain standards of literary and intellectual taste which, while they neither guarantee originality nor contribute to power of thought, at least prevent a thinker from making a fool of himself. They ensure that even when what he says is false, it is at least respectably false; that even when it is nonsense, it is the right kind of nonsense. Just as a first-rate musical critic turned musical composer will be saved by his experience from the composition of music which is palpably vulgar and trivial, and produce respectably competent work or none at all, so a mind which is impregnated with the best of the thought of its predecessors and contemporaries will be automatically educated up to a level of critical taste at which the production of pretentious banality in the name of philosophy will be impossible.

Qualifications of the Philosopher. (*iii*) *Ability to Think.* Thirdly, there must be a capacity for sustained and coherent thinking. The mind, in fact, must be able to reason. To reason is not merely to assert but to produce grounds for one's assertion. It is to show that B is true *because* A is true, that B in fact *follows* from A. 'Thus' and 'hence' and 'therefore'; 'is followed by', 'the conclusion is', 'the evidence suggests', are the words and phrases that one should expect to find in a chain of reasoning. Lacking these, the would-be philosophy becomes a series of announcements devoid of authority save such as is conferred by the conviction of the announcer; it is a mere saying of things.

Now this power of sustained reasoning is to a large extent acquired. A clear head is no doubt a natural endowment, and, lacking it, no amount of exercise and training will enable a man to think clearly. But equally no mind, however clear, unless it is developed by exercise and training, can think fruitfully. Just as grammar supplies the rules of speech, so logic supplies those of thought. No doubt a mind untrained in logic will by long and patient endeavour discover some of these rules for itself, just as a company of children brought up by deaf mutes will sooner or later evolve rules of grammatical speech for itself. But I cannot see what is gained by encouraging every mind to make afresh for itself the discoveries which its predecessors have made for it. My business friends would never dream of permitting their children to discover the rules of arithmetic unaided, still less of engaging a clerk who had made up an arithmetic for himself. They insist that their children and clerks shall equip themselves for the business of getting on in the world by acquiring the elementary accomplishment of ciphering. Why then should they presume to undertake the more arduous labour of abstract thinking without subjecting their minds to the equivalent discipline of logic? That individual spontaneity should not be overladen with the weight of other men's knowledge is no doubt important. But it is equally important that the instrument of individual thinking should be sharpened by training along the lines which others have laid down.

Digressive Protest against the 'New Education'. There is perceptible to-day a salutary reaction against the extreme libertarianism of the 'New Education'. Ten years ago advanced educationalists refused to instruct either the minds or the morals of their children. 'The vilest abortionist', Shaw had said, 'is he who attempts to mould a child's character,' and wishing not to impede the free development of their charges, teachers took a pride in withholding instruction in matters of fact and guidance in matters of morals. Children were not only to discover for themselves the fundamental principles of science and geometry, even, it would seem, the fundamental rules of Latin and French grammar; they were also to determine their own conduct, to solve for themselves their moral problems. To-day many have come to see that this procedure imposes upon the child's mind a strain which it is incapable of bearing, by forcing upon it the necessity of decisions which it is unfitted to make.

To require a young mind to decide every question for itself upon merits is unfair. It has neither the data nor the equipment for such decision. In practice it becomes strained, in extreme cases exhausted, by this obligation which the eccentric libertarianism of its parents has laid upon it, and the faculties of judgment and decision are weakened instead of strengthened by being called into play before their time. A child who is allowed to make all its mistakes for itself, with nobody but itself to blame for making them, must continuously meet disaster. The world will appear to such a one as a place where the exercise of continuous care is necessary, if one is to avoid discomfiture, and the most apparently innocuous actions produce the most disconcerting and disproportionate results.

Moreover, the child, having no one to grumble at but himself, loses one of childhood's most reliable compensations, the fun of blaming 'grown-ups'.

These are only some of the results which follow from

wilfully depriving children of the accumulated wisdom of the race in the form of moral instruction and practical guidance in the art of living. To tell a child at the outset that there are certain things which as a requirement of practical wisdom it must, certain things which it must not do, if it does not want to be punished, is not to cramp its spontaneity or to abort its character; it is to save it an immense amount of trouble in finding out what these things are for itself. Similarly, to insist that those who undertake the task of speculating at large about the universe should acquaint themselves in advance with the fact that there are certain things which as a matter of logical necessity one must not think, certain things which one must, is at once to save them the trouble of making for themselves all the mistakes which thinkers have made in the past, and to protect their work from the unmitigated contempt of thinkers in the present. Such acquaintance is made in the study of logic and of the history of philosophy. These studies admittedly are not a royal road to truth, but they do constitute a safeguard against straying down *every* by-road of error.

Qualifications of the Philosopher. (iv) The Art of Exposition. Fourthly, there is needful some skill in the art of exposition. Those who are not content with truth when they have found it but feel constrained to communicate it to others must learn how to express themselves. The need for clarity of expression is nowhere greater than in philosophy. Philosophy is bound from its very nature to be difficult and obscure. But its obscurity may be due to one or other of two different causes. There is the expression of obscurity, and there is obscurity of expression. The former is pardonable; it is probably inevitable. There is no necessary reason—at least I am aware of none—why the nature of the universe should be such as to be readily comprehensible by the intelligences of twentieth-century Nordic adults, and those who see further into it than their fellows are bound, when they come to report what they have seen, to appear obscure to their fellows. But obscurity of expression is simply another name for bad craftsmanship. A thinker who wishes to be understood should study to make himself understandable. He should learn the art of clear and concise statement, and never use long and esoteric words when his meaning can be conveyed equally well by short, familiar ones. He should not hesitate to make a copious use of metaphor and simile, he should illustrate continuously by means of concrete examples, and he should never talk about any subject without first explaining why he is proposing to talk about it, which means, among other things, indicating its relevance to the subject about which he has just been talking.

Vested Interests in Philosophy. Many professional philosophers, it must be admitted, habitually neglect these rules. Particularly do philosophical lecturers, who, one might have supposed, would, since it is after all their profession, make a special study of the art of lucid expression, neglect them. Philosophical lecturers are for the most part intolerably obscure; they have a horror of illustrating their reasoning by examples, and the unnecessary technicality of the terms they habitually employ suggests a Trade Unionist's disinclination to disclose to outsiders the secrets of his craft, by allowing them to suppose that it can be practised by persons who have not first received technical instruction in its mysteries. If it were once conceded that philosophy could be usefully pursued by those unlearned in the jargon of philosophers, the prestige and in the long run the selling value of philosophy would diminish. There is a vested interest in philosophy as in everything else, and its maintenance depends upon nobody being allowed to dispel the myth that the difficulty of philosophy is so extreme, that it is only by invoking and incidentally paying for the assistance of professional philosophers that the uninitiated can hope to understand it.

When professional philosophers so often set a bad example, it is not to be expected that business men, whose systems are attacked by philosophy, in their years of retirement, will set a better.

The Blight of Obscurity. Nor do they. The lucubrations of my friends which have caused me so much embarrassment have been for the most part meaningless. Meaninglessness, indeed, has been their most embarrassing quality. If a meaning is clear, you can at least make up your mind whether it seems to you to be right or wrong; and, even if wrong, what there is to be said in its favour. And warmed by your host's dinner, mellowed by his wine, you say it. I can make shift to say a good word on behalf even of nonsense, provided that I know what sort of nonsense it is. But if I do not? If the writer's intentions are so completely obscured by his mode of expressing them, that it is impossible to discover what they are, then in seeking to encourage I may do just the reverse, praising a monist for his dualism, a spiritualist for his materialism, a transcendentalist for his immanentism, and a believer in any and every available cult and 'ism' for the forthrightness of his general scepticism.

I do not wish to be thought to suggest that there was *in fact* some undiscerned core of rational meaning in the productions to which I have referred. I do not think that there was. My hosts' conversation on metaphysical topics, which sooner or later in the evening they would infallibly open, precluded any such supposition. Their written lucubrations were, I suspect, nothing but the froth of ill-stored and inadvisably stirred minds. But even if there had been, it would have been so smothered beneath the grandiose and swelling utterances of the writer, that, so far at least as I was concerned, it would have remained undetected. And so, the most exasperating thing about the whole sorry business is the half-thought, of which I can never quite rid myself, that there may have been something in these productions after all. Just one grain of truth, perhaps, in one of them! It is not much to ask and I could wish that it were so. But my reason, instinct, training, education, critical sense, every faculty whether natural or acquired, that I possess, combine to assure me that it is not so.

IV

Christian Scientists. And now, lest my readers should feel that all this is a beating of the air, that I am making too much of the belittling of the critical reason and of the intellectual excesses which such belittling has engendered, I propose to edify them with a concrete example. After due consideration, I have chosen the Bible of the Christian Scientists, *Science and Health*, which, prepared by Mrs. Eddy some time in the last century, is now reverently read in thousands of Christian Science churches every Sunday morning.

Christian Science—it is a commonplace—makes its converts by the thousands. I do not know what manner of people its clientèle may be in America, the country of origin, but in big English industrial towns such as Leeds or Manchester, it attracts numbers of middle and lower middle class people, who believe themselves to be superior in intelligence and culture to the average of those classes. They have, perhaps, some knowledge of comparative religion, or of the Higher Criticism of the Bible. In consequence they are ready to assure you that all the religions of the world contain the same fundamental truths, and that Christianity, in so far as under the influence of the Church it has gone beyond these truths, has wandered into superstition, myth and error. For the fundamental truths they are prepared to contend with enthusiasm. With the light of evangelism in their eyes they assure you that spirit alone is real, matter an illusion; and cheerfully write you off not only as a fool too dull to see the truth, but as a sinner too lost to embrace it when it is pointed out to you, if you venture to question this assurance. As for pain, it is either glorified or explained away.

The official textbook of the cult, Mrs. Eddy's *Science and Health*, from which every Sunday the same extracts are read in every Christian Science church throughout the world, consists of selected passages from the Bible, followed by passages of comment by Mrs. Eddy. No unofficial word, whether in the form of sermon or of extemporary prayer, is uttered at a Christian Science service. Thus the fallible human element is eliminated and members of the congregation are enabled to assure you that everything you hear during the service, being either Bible or Eddy, owns a supernatural source.

And what *do* you hear?

'*Scientific Statement of Being*.' From the official textbook I have selected one or two of the more fundamental assertions. I propose to lay them before you. The first is entitled 'Scientific Statement of Being':

'*There is no life, truth, intelligence nor substance in matter. All is infinite Mind and its infinite manifestations, for God is all in all. Spirit is immortal Truth; matter is mortal error. Spirit is the real and eternal; matter is the unreal and temporal. Spirit is God, and man is His image and likeness. Therefore, man is not material; he is spiritual.*'

This initial statement will give some idea of the intellectual content of the whole. I content myself with two

preliminary observations before commenting in a little
more detail.

First, what I have quoted is a pronouncement, not an
argument. It is a succession of unsupported statements.
No grounds are given for any of these statements, except
for the last, when the blessed word 'therefore' is introduced once to lead up to the conclusion that man is not
material, *because* he is made in God's image and God is
spirit. The presumption behind this 'therefore' is, I take
it, that the premise 'man is made in God's image' is
more certain, or at least more obvious, than the conclusion 'man is not material'. For this reason, the second
statement is considered to *follow from* the first. Since this
is the only argument used, it seems a pity that it should
be such a bad one. That I am made in God's image is,
of course, possible; but it does not seem to me to be
nearly so certain as that I have teeth. Now teeth certainly appear to be material; nor is any good argument
adduced for convincing me that they are not. The
correct form of the argument should therefore be: 'I
possess teeth; in some sense, indeed, I *am* my teeth, as I
realize only too well when they ache: teeth are material;
therefore I cannot be made in God's image, unless He
also has teeth and is material.'

Secondly, if 'God is All', there cannot be anything but
God. Therefore, there cannot be matter, and there cannot be a false belief that there is matter. (The possibilities that matter is a *part* of God is, I suppose, ruled out
by the further statement that 'God is Spirit'.) Now
it is of course the case that, even if there was no

matter, I could falsely believe that there was. But I cannot falsely believe that there is matter, if there is no such thing as false belief. Therefore, not only is matter an illusion, but nobody falsely believes matter to be real. In fact, there is nobody to believe anything except God, since 'God is All'. Why, then, one cannot help asking, all this fuss?

Error and Sin. Why, in particular, the heartburning over error and sin and the threat of punishment for error. For consider the following:

'*Punishment of Error.*

'*We acknowledge God's forgiveness of sin in the destruction of sin and the spiritual understanding that casts out evil as unreal. But the belief in sin is punishable so long as the belief lasts.*'

This remarkable assertion prompts the following questions. (1) If there is only God, what is meant by talking about evil and error? Do these exist in addition to God? Presumably not. Are they parts of God? Certainly not. Are they illusions? Yes, they are!

But (2) if there is only God, how can there be illusions? Can God's mind create and nourish them? No. Can mine? I think that it can. But, if it can, my mind must be other than God's, and all is not God.

Moreover (3) I certainly believe that I suffer and that men do me evil. This belief, I am assured, is a delusion, since 'evil is unreal', and so is suffering. Therefore, in believing as I do, I am making a mistake. Is the mistake real or not? Clearly real, since, if the mistake were itself illusory, it would not be *really* false to hold that I *really* suffer and that men *really* do me evil. If it were not *really* false to hold this, then my belief that I suffer and that men do me evil would stand, and evil and pain would be real. The mistake, then, cannot *itself* be illusory. It follows that the mistake must be real, real in whatever sense of the word 'real' evil and pain are asserted to be other than 'real'. It seems, therefore, that we cannot escape the view that there must be 'real' error in the world, if we wish to eliminate from it 'real' pain and evil.

But (4) can we in fact eliminate them? Let us suppose, to take a topical example, that a German pacifist, socialist who does not believe that war is the most satisfactory method of settling international disputes, and who is inclined to regard the present economic organization of society as in certain respects regrettable, is beaten up by young men, fired by counter-revolutionary enthusiasm. He is, let us say, beaten with leather riding whips and steel rods which curl round his face, break his cheekbones and smash his right eye. The force of the blows presently renders him unconscious. His assailants, still pursuing their efforts to convince him of the error of his ways and opinions by endearing to him their own, restore him to consciousness by applying lighted cigarette ends to the soles of his feet and matches to his beard and moustache. When he is again conscious and they are assured of his renewed ability to feel, the whole process is repeated *da capo*.

Now, speaking for myself, I am convinced that the

pacifist in question suffers pain and that he is the victim of evil, of the evil, namely, of cruelty, which seems to me to be the worst of all sins. Christian Science doctrine assures me that, since this belief is false, I am, in holding it, myself sinning, and warns me that I shall in due course be punished for my sin.

Difficulties in the Doctrine of Sin and Evil. I am naturally not anxious to accept this assurance, and it is not without satisfaction that I find it exposed to the following difficulties:

(1) There is the absurdity of asking us to suppose (a) that the philosopher is not really being hurt, but falsely thinks that he is; (b) that his assailants are not really intending to do him evil, but that they only think that they are. Personally I am far more certain that both the existence of pain and the existence of cruelty are facts than I can be of the truth of any train of argument which seeks to assure me that they are not. Even if it were divinely revealed to Mrs. Eddy that they are not, a revelation asserted to have been made to somebody else in the past cannot, in the absence of any evidence in its favour, possibly be as convincing to the assailed philosopher as the certainty of the present feeling of pain in himself.

(2) (a) Although sin is unreal, the belief in sin is, we are told, punishable 'so long as the belief lasts'. There can be no punishment by a just God for that which is not wrong. We cannot, then, suppose that the belief that sin is real is not itself a sin. Now this belief as held, for

example, by myself, is certainly real; I really do believe that cruelty is a sin. The belief that sin is not real is, then, it would seem, an exception to the view that sin is not real.

(b) If the belief that pain is real and cruelty a sin is itself a sin, we reach the conclusion that when A tortures B for his own sadistic amusement, the sinner is not A but B, since B sins by falsely thinking that A hurts him. This conclusion seems to me frankly absurd. Moreover, how is B to be cured of his sin? As long as he believes he is being wilfully hurt by A, he will, we are told, be punished for his false belief in A's sin and his own pain. What form will this punishment take? Presumably, that of suffering, either physical or mental. I at least can conceive of punishment in no other terms. This further suffering the unfortunate B will still insist on considering to be real—if he did not think it real, it would not be suffering, and would not, therefore, punish—and, so considering, would repeat his sin of holding sin to be real. This repeated sin would again deserve punishment, and so on *ad infinitum*. It seems difficult, therefore, to see how anyone can ever reach 'the spiritual understanding that casts out evil as unreal'.

(3) *The Doctrine that Pain is Unreal.* Whatever we may think of 'sin' and 'evil', which owing to the ambiguity of these expressions may be interpreted in any one of a number of different senses, some one of which might conceivably render the statements quoted from the Christian Science Bible not *absolutely* absurd, the doc-

trine that pain is unreal seems to me to be so immeasurably silly, that I cannot bring myself to dignify it further with serious comment. In this respect I find myself in agreement with an esteemed contemporary of mine at Oxford who, at the close of a long and exhausting scholarship examination lasting over four days, was asked to write a three-hour essay on the thesis propounded by the Stoics: 'The good man can be happy even on the rack.' Irritated by the foolishness of the remark, and determining by one magnificent gesture finally to dispel his not very rosy chances of obtaining the scholarship, he commented briefly: 'If the man was a very good man, and the rack was a very bad rack, this might be true. Otherwise not!' and handed in his paper. The comment seems to me to be final.

But it is the metaphysical rather than the ethical doctrines of Christian Science which I wish chiefly to commend to the attention of the readers of this chapter, not because they are either more or less foolish, but because they are more relevant to its main theme, the effects of metaphysics upon weak heads. I append, therefore, a final quotation on 'matter'.

Mrs. Eddy on 'Matter'. Suspecting that this word was being used in a number of surprising senses, I looked it up in the glossary of terms at the end of Mrs. Eddy's book, and found it defined as follows:

'*Matter: Mortality; another name for mortal mind; illusion; intelligence; substance and life in non-intelligence and mortality;*

life resulting in death and death in life; sensation in the sensationless; mind originating in matter; the opposite of truth; the opposite of spirit; the opposite of God; that of which immortal Mind takes no cognizance; that which the world mind sees, hears, tastes and smells only in belief.'

Truly a formidable definition, and, when we remember that it describes an illusion, a surprising one. You have forgotten that matter is an illusion? Please to bear in mind that 'God is All'. Now matter is 'the opposite of God'. But if God is All, there can be no opposite to Him. Therefore, that which is said to be His opposite, cannot exist.

Why, then, you naturally wonder, say all these things about it? Or what in the name of clarity and common sense can the author of this ethico-religious, uplifting twaddle be about, when she ascribes all these characteristics to something that, on her own showing, does not exist; when she so laboriously defines what is not? I do not know. Nor is my bewilderment lightened by discovering that, although matter is an illusion, known not really but 'only in belief', it can nevertheless produce certain highly important effects.

For example, under the heading '*This material body we have accepted*', I read 'We are all essential to God'. 'The universe is governed by perfect laws like mathematics'; 'Matter'—we conclude with the usual dig at matter— 'Matter is an illusion'. These, we are told, are familiar truths. Why, then do we not recognize them?

Because: 'The material standpoint hides [them] from

us.' Also: 'The material existence sometimes gets us down.' Matter, then, although an illusion, is sufficiently real to prevent us from realizing that it is an illusion. It also 'gets us down'. Now this is really very odd. Either matter is real, or else it is not. If it is real, it must be God, since God is 'All in all'. We also, if we are real —and Mrs. Eddy does not suggest that we are not— are parts of God. Now that God should hide truths from us, that is to say, from parts of Himself, seems very odd. Also how does God 'get Himself down'?

If, on the other hand, matter is not real, how can it possibly hide anything or depress anyone? If it be said that it is only our *false belief* in it that hides and depresses, there are the difficulties first, that there must be something to account for this universal false belief—it is inconceivable that all minds should wilfully but unanimously invent *the same error* for themselves, if there was absolutely nothing to account for it—and, secondly, that insistence on the reality of the false belief in matter results, as I have already noted, merely in the substitution of real error for real matter. You cannot, in fact, postulate God or Spirit as the only reality and everything else as an illusion, without giving some account of the source of the illusion.

Scolding of Christian Science. The plain fact is, of course, that there are numberless individual minds which believe that pain and evil occur and that matter is real. Christian Scientists, while holding officially that 'God is All', nevertheless treat their own individual minds both as real and as individual, making their Church out of them and addressing their propaganda to them. They then proceed to dismiss most of the universally held beliefs of the minds in question as illusory, without giving any reasons in favour of this wholesale dismissal or any account of the origin of the illusions.

When pressed they take refuge in a cloud of words, identifying matter with 'mortal mind', yet defining it as 'sensation in the sensationless', thus blandly denying mind its most obvious distinguishing capacity, the capacity for receiving sensations; postulating a God who knows everything, yet telling us that His 'Immortal mind takes no cognizance' of matter; assuring us that 'Immortal Mind' is everything, yet, without a word of explanation, asking us to accept the existence of minds which are mortal; defining matter as the opposite of truth, spirit and God, as if there were no difficulty in supposing God, truth and spirit to be identical; predicating matter as real in order the better to denounce it as unreal, and committing every conceivable solecism that the maggot of faith can breed in the womb of intellectual incompetence.

I cannot bear further to soil the perfection of these things with comment. I content myself with remarking that it is only an age which has seen the twilight not only of religion but of reason that could have given birth to a creed that combines the worst features of both, using reason without precision to support a faith without dignity.

Chapter II

Defence of Value—I. Value in the Modern World

★

Chartres Cathedral. That Chartres Cathedral is one of the most glorious sights that rejoices the eye of man few will be found to deny. It is, indeed, a miracle of loveliness. It is of great size and towering height; yet, so perfect is the proportioning of its parts, that it appears of only moderate dimensions even to a 'close up' view. It looks, for example, no larger than Winchester cathedral, much smaller than St. Paul's. It is, says the guide book, the most perfect monument that the Middle Ages have bequeathed to posterity. I am quite ready to believe it.

The cathedral is encircled on the outside with the faces and figures not only of angels and saints, but of devils; hundreds of devils, and of the most grotesque shapes, thrusting their malignant countenances from the numberless parapets and buttresses to threaten or to leer at an indifferent world. At least, it is indifferent to-day. We do not now believe in the reality of objective evil; and after a casual glance at the devils we glance away again, too busy with our sightseeing to meditate upon the mood of their makers. If we spare them a second look, it is only to laugh at their hideousness. For the Middle Ages, I suppose, they were real enough, visible emblems of the powers of darkness, which were believed to be as integral a part of the constitution of the universe as those of goodness and of light. Why were they featured in a temple to their enemies, God and His angels? Partly, perhaps, in propitiation, partly in scorn. The intention, it may well have been, was to humiliate them by giving them positions ludicrous, undignified or obscure. The suggestion is the merest guesswork. So far is the mood of the sculptors of the Middle Ages from our modern comprehension, that to speculate upon their motives is idle. It is enough that we should have their work. And their work, I repeat, is lovely. What is most remarkable is the combination of simplicity and complexity. It is not that a balance has been struck; the two modes, the simplicity, the complexity, exist side by side; yet neither interferes with the effect of the other. On the one hand there are the bare, stark outlines of the southern tower; on the other the infinite multiplicity of detail of the northern, a multiplicity which extends over the cathedral as a whole, so that looking down upon the maze of turrets, gargoyles, statues, pillars, buttresses, arches and parapets, one seems less to be regarding a single building than a whole city in which nothing would be easier than for the stranger to lose his way. Yet the com plexity never degenerates into a muddle. By some miracle form is retained, and the infinitely numerous details fall effortlessly into their places as parts of an integrated whole.

I. Value in the Modern World

Within are solemnity and grandeur. Immense pillars soar to the decorated roof, and the many windows of highly coloured glass diffuse a light, dim but incredibly rich, over the vast interior. Chartres Cathedral is a monument to the glory of the human spirit; like a Bach fugue or a Mozart quartet it bears witness to all that the human spirit might be, would like to be, in its most optimistic moments conceives that it will be, and in practice, alas, so rarely is. Rarely, and as the centuries go by, it would seem, increasingly rarely.

Aeroplane Sheds. On the hill opposite the cathedral across the river valley, along which the houses of the old town are strung, there is an aerodrome. Enormous tin shapes, the homes of the aeroplanes, squat hugely upon the flat top of the down. A line of poles connected by wires runs along its edge. The grass is gashed and rutted, the hillside littered with refuse, while hoardings and enamel signs advertising drinks and cosmetics sprout from the outraged earth. Up the side of this hill creep rows of new houses strung out singly along the road, or clotting into patches of angry pink. The whole hillside with its formless sprawl of tin and brass and harsh new tiling is like a shout, a shout which is a continuous embodied insult to the lovely building which stands opposite. Meanwhile the aeroplanes roar and swoop impartially over the twentieth century and the twelfth, circling round the towers of the cathedral and rending the peace which has immemorially surrounded it.

The Twentieth Century and the Twelfth

The Twentieth Century and the Twelfth. In this ganglion of vulgarity and ugliness which fronts the beauty of the cathedral there is a note of deliberate defiance. It is exactly as if a small and dirty boy, unable to respond to beauty save by a feeling of vague discomfort—here is something which, he feels, he cannot understand, yet resents, resents because he is conscious that it belittles him, making him feel small and cheap and vulgar—is moved to assert his independence and to recover his self-respect by cocking snooks at what discomfits him. But although he cannot understand, he can destroy. I visited Chartres on the 13th July. In preparation for the fête upon the fourteenth a fleet of aeroplanes was rehearsing a demonstration. The cathedral was at once the base and the target of their operations. Arranged in three squadrons they flew over and round it, circled the towers, descended almost to the ground before the West front and then in echelon formation climbed slowly up its face.

As a symbol of power the demonstration was prodigious. Any single bomb dropped from any one of the so easily circling planes would, it was sufficiently obvious, reduce the cathedral to ruins. As a manifestation of taste it was, one felt, less impressive. Detonating and erupting as they postured before that magnificent edifice, the aeroplanes constituted the appropriate, the final comment of the twentieth century upon the twelfth. It was natural and inevitable for the men of the twelfth century to build what was beautiful; it is, it seems, natural and inevitable for our own generation to construct what is ugly. I do not mean that we cannot build beautifully, if we please; but we so rarely do please. Beauty, indeed, is not for us an obvious, an overriding consideration. We are concerned with speed, with cheapness, with efficiency, and we attain them; but with beauty we are not concerned. And the result is that whenever some typical product of the twentieth century confronts us side by side with a monument of the past, we cannot avoid being humiliated by the contrast.

That you may realize it to the full, travel to Oxford by train. The first glimpse of the city reveals the dreaming spires celebrated by poets and guide books and vulgarized in innumerable picture postcards. As you draw nearer, you see first an outer scurf of staring pink villas, and then the yellow dinginess of the mean buildings that surround the station; the first is the typical expression of the twentieth, the second of the nineteenth century. In the middle there stands still intact the core of grey buildings which has made the loveliness of Oxford famous, but the core is engirt by ever-deepening rings of meanness and squalor, as successive generations leave their mark upon the city.

Beauty and its Lack in Stone, Sound and Words. If we look at the buildings of the Cotswolds, at an Essex village, at a Queen Anne country house, or at Chartres Cathedral, and then compare them with the typical products of this age and the last, petrol pumps and garages, bungalows and railway stations, miners' cottages and national schools, gas works and power stations and rich men's 'follies', we must, I think, concede that ours is not an age that expresses itself easily in visual beauty.

Nor in audible. There was a period comprising the major part of the seventeenth and the first half of the eighteenth century, when a musician had only to set pen to paper to compose something which would at least not outrage a critical taste, which was at least reasonably good. Almost all the first-rate music of the world was composed during a period of about a hundred and fifty years from 1685, when Bach, Handel and Scarlatti were born, to 1828 when Schubert died. But in addition to the great men, the good second-raters produced music that was worth more than all that has been written since the period ended, while the ordinary hack men writing decent, presentable stuff were as thick as blackberries in September. Our own age is so poor in creative artists that, if none of the sounds made since Schubert died were ever to be heard again, I for one should not care a row of semiquavers.

As with sound and stone, so also with words. Everybody more or less in fifth-century Athens seems to have written reasonably well; everybody more or less in Elizabethan England and in eighteenth-century France; the Augustans wrote well enough; the Victorians produced a round dozen of first-rate poets and half a dozen supreme novelists. Compared with the literature of these favoured periods, our own is poverty stricken. If you want to know precisely how poverty stricken, read those corroding books of literary appraisement, or rather of literary denigration by F.R. and Q. Leavis. We have

I. Value in the Modern World

of course our big men; we have Shaw and Wells from the immediate past; we have Virginia Woolf, Joyce and, I should like to add, Forster in the present. But compared with the enormous bulk of the writing public, the first-rank writers are negligible. Never before, as Mrs. Leavis has pointed out, were there so many writers; never has the proportion of great ones to the rest been so low. In short, this is no more an age of great literature than it is an age of great music, great painting or great architecture. The fact is, and the admission may as well be made now as later, that, taking us by and large, we do not produce beauty. Why not? Partly, I suggest, because we do not appreciate it when we meet it, or miss it when we do not; because, in fact, we are not concerned with it one way or the other.

Twentieth-Century Ideals. Our ideals lie in other directions. They are mainly bound up with the movement of pieces of matter. So far as those pieces of matter which are our own bodies are concerned, we desire not only that they should be moved but moved quickly. Hence the modern cult of speed. The distinctively modern use which we make of our bodies is to cause them to be transported as frequently as possible and as rapidly as possible from place to place. In regard to inorganic pieces of matter, we enjoy and admire the rapid displacement at controlled speeds and in specified directions of small round pieces of matter by long thin ones in the shape of mallets, bats, cues, clubs, sticks and rackets; also by leather boots. For the rest we amuse ourselves with the pursuit of sport, which is the name we give to the introduction of small pieces of metal from a safe distance into the bodies of defenceless birds and beasts, and exhaust ourselves in the pursuit of wealth, which we desire mainly in order that we may expend it in the accumulation of the largest possible number of complex material objects, such as houses, refrigerators, radio sets, porcelain baths, telephones, motor cars, pieces of shining metal, coloured stones, and, if we are persons of high culture, articles of 'virtu' such as 'old masters', Chippendale furniture, or Spode china.

In this way material things, their movement and their accumulation come to dominate our lives and to form the ideals of our leisure. And these ideals are cultivated not, as one might have been tempted to suppose, for the sake of any of the traditional ends of human activity, because of the happiness they bring, the beauty they create, the truth they make plain, the good they do, but for their own sweet selves.

The Cult of Speed. Consider, for example, our addiction to the rapid conveyance of our bodies in petrol-propelled mechanisms over the surface of the earth. If two men leave Manchester for Bettws-y-Coed and the one drives so gently that not a single speck of dust on a pedestrian's shoe is disturbed, while the other drives so vigorously that he leaves a trail of frightened humanity along the whole route, what margin separates the pair at their journey's end in Wales? Fifteen minutes! And how does the speed devotee spend that quarter of an hour which he has stolen from the clasp of inexorable Time? He lounges, all liver and no legs, in the bar a little longer before he feeds, consumes an extra cocktail, toys with a few stale magazines, grumbles that his food is not ready, brags a little about his driving. . . . The world suffers through his speed; and it suffers to no noble purpose. If he were a surgeon hastening to a purulent appendix, we could bear with him. If he were a lover fresh home from the Indies yearning to meet his bride, we could bear with him. If he obtained any real or lasting satisfaction from his speed debauch, his conduct, although still intolerable, would be at least excusable. But he does not. He is just a fool in a hurry. He has no possible defence for his folly, and we know it as well as he knows it.

Amusements of the Fortunate. With no obligation but to promote the satisfaction of their devotees, the final criticism of the ideals of the modern world is that they fail to satisfy. Consider for a moment the habits of the unemployed rich who, possessing not only the money but the leisure to gratify their tastes, epitomize in their pursuits the ideals of our civilization. You will find them engaged in enjoyment *tout court* on the Riviera, where there exists an industry for the sole purpose of providing with amusements those who cannot amuse themselves. Those engaged in this industry proceed on the supposition that the temperament of rich and idle persons is equivalent to that of small, spoilt children. Since, however, they are in years adults, a circumstance which makes it impracticable to force them to do things by beating them, and, since in order to escape the demon of boredom they must nevertheless do things, the object of this industry is to create in them the impression that they are discovering interesting and important things to do for themselves. It is a fundamental principle among those engaged in inventing occupations for the rich to discover for themselves that they can never stand any amusement for more than an hour. Before the hour is over they become bored and, like spoilt children tiring of their toys, must be amused with something else. They spend an hour in sunbathing, an hour at a motor rally, an hour at polo, an hour at cocktails and reading the papers in the sun. The theatre thoughtfully provides long intervals so that people may gamble as a relief from watching the play, and there is dancing as a relief from gambling. They have a particular penchant on the Riviera for shooting half-blinded pigeons. For my part, I do not find it surprising that the suicide rate among the unemployed rich is the highest of any class of the community.

Introduction of Absolute Values. Personally—and I hope that it will not set the reader against me—I take an old-fashioned view of the issues raised by the Riviera concept of the 'good time'. I believe that the universe contains certain elements or factors which are uniquely and absolutely valuable. And when I say that they are absolutely valuable, I mean among other things—although this is not all that I mean—first, that they are desired for their own sake and not for the sake of any further good that may accrue from their pursuit or possession; and, secondly, that they would remain valuable, even if nobody desired them.

That there must be some things which are desired for their own sake is, I think, tolerably plain. Conceive that on a particular occasion I desire something, desire it, that is to say, in relation to some special purpose that I wish to serve, to some end that I have in view. I have a cold, or believe that I am about to have a cold and desire quinine. 'Quinine', I say, 'is *good* for a cold. I want some quinine.' Now nobody supposes that I want quinine for its own sweet sake; I desire it for the sake of something else. What else? In order that it may confer immunity from colds. But immunity from colds is not desired by me for its own sake. It is too negative, too limited an ideal. I desire, then, to be immune from colds for some ulterior reason because, let us say, I want health, and, so long as I have or am liable to have a cold, I cannot be healthy. Why, then, do I desire health? At this point I may introduce an absolute value; I may say that I desire health for its own sake, because I intuitively perceive health to be something which is good in itself and which requires, therefore, neither justification nor commendation—if you can't, I may answer a sceptic, *see* that health is a good thing, then I have no more to say to you. Or I may hold that health in *itself* is of no value; it is valuable only because of the use I make of it, or because of the greater energy and efficiency it confers, or because it is a *sine qua non* of happiness.

Why, then, do I desire energy or efficiency or happiness? Energy might be valued because the energetic man wins power or fame. Do I, then, desire power or fame for themselves? Possibly, possibly not! But, if not, if I give the answer that I do not desire these things in and for themselves, I shall always find myself committed to some further object of desire as a means to which these things, which I do not desire *merely* for themselves, are regarded as conducive, and, because conducive, therefore desirable. And obviously I must stop somewhere. Some things, it is obvious, must be desired for themselves alone; some things must be recognized as uniquely and ultimately valuable, so that, were we to achieve them— not that we ever do—we should not then find ourselves led on to some further thing which they helped to bring within our grasp, but should rest and be content with them. Such things I call absolute values, or ultimate values.

The Universe of Science. The judgment of mankind— based, we must suppose, upon its experience—has fined down the number of these things which are ultimately valuable in themselves to three, Truth, Goodness and Beauty, to which I think a further, Happiness, should probably be added. Truth, Goodness and Beauty are the dowagers of philosophy. At this moment, in common with most dowagers they are under a cloud. It is commonly urged that the so-called absolute and objective values are neither absolute nor objective; that they are subjective figments projected by the mind of man upon

the empty canvas of a valueless universe. Mrs. Grundy
in the nineteenth century was regarded as a real person;
to-day she is regarded as the personification of the envy
of elderly females seeking to deter their youngers from
the enjoyments denied to themselves by their lack of
charm. Similarly with the Dowagers. Mrs. Grundy is
presented as an embodied figment of prohibition; *they*
are the embodied figments of consolation; of consolation
and of assurance.

The universe revealed by science is, we know, immeasurably huge; it is also, so far as we can tell, completely lifeless. In the vast immensities of geological
space and astronomical time life seems like a tiny glow,
flickering uncertainly for a while but doomed ultimately
to extinction, so soon as the material conditions which
gave it birth cease to obtain. One day the sun will either
collide with another star, or go out. When that catastrophe happens, life will cease to be. Meanwhile it
strays an unwanted and incidental passenger across a
fundamentally hostile environment, an environment in
which the alien and the brutal conditions and underlies
the friendly and the spiritual.

Such are the outlines of the universe sketched by
science. And, frankly, we find it intolerable; so intolerable, that we are driven to clothe the universe with the
whimsies of our imagination in order to be able to
assure ourselves that its *physical* appearance is not all.
It is not the whole of reality, it is not even reality at all, for
behind it, we argue, there must be something which is
spiritual and akin to ourselves, something which, once

conceived in our own immediate image as God, has to-
day with the growth of sophistication been depersonal-
ized—do we not pride ourselves upon our emancipation
from the gross anthropomorphism of savages?—into the
three Dowagers. The Dowagers, then, are not objective
factors in the universe; they are emanations projected
by the mind of man. So the scientists explaining, and
not only explaining but explaining away, value. . . .

Subjectivism in the Climate of the Age. So also my students,
at least the more intelligent of them who, coming to
philosophy classes with a stock of ideas which embody
what they believe to be the conclusions of modern science,
but which in fact represent the petrified science of some
fifty years ago, unhesitatingly assume and aggressively
assert first, that only material things exist and are real;
secondly, that beauty and truth are only ideas in the
mind of man; and thirdly, that the mind of man is probably only a camouflaged version of his brain. Any argument to the contrary is received with suspicion as tending to bolster up that *démodé* superstition, supernatural
Christianity, as derogatory to science, and as unbecom-
ing the dignity of the rational mind.

I ask them whether, if the number three is only an
idea in the human mind, twice three would cease to
make six, if nobody knew that it made six. I ask them
why, if beauty is *merely* a quality which the mind projects, it projects it into some things, pictures for example,
and not into others such as pieces of string. Does not this,
I ask, suggest the possession *in its own right* by the object

into which beauty is 'projected' of some quality which stimulates the projection? What account, then, are we to give of this independent, objective, stimulating quality which is possessed by the object in its own right? Is it not perhaps, precisely the quality which men have wished to designate by the name of 'beauty'? I ask also whether, if the quality of beauty is 'projected' or imputed by the mind, the quality of squareness is also imputed by the mind. If it is, do they believe that chessboards are not *really* square. If it is not, on what principle do they propose to distinguish between the one quality and the other? As to matter, which is alone asserted to be really real, I ask them what precisely, in the light of modern physics, they think matter is? If their view that matter alone is real is correct, that view must itself be real. What sort of matter then, is the view that only matter is real? Or that seven times seven make forty-nine? And so on, and so on. . . .

The methods by which students are discomfited will not be particularly interesting to my readers, who are not likely to be as simple as my students. What is interesting is the fact that the views in question receive countenance not only from the science of fifty years ago, but from the most widely read authors of to-day; for example, from Aldous Huxley, the guide, philosopher and friend of the intelligent, modern young, whom my students frequently quote in their support. Huxley's horror of absolutes and values, his dislike of any kind of objectivity is, indeed, so characteristic of the age that I propose in this and subsequent chapters to examine in some little detail his utterances on the subject, taking them as typical of much modern thought.

Preliminary Appearance of Aldous Huxley. I have, for example, dealt in the fourth chapter of this book with the philosophical implications of Huxley's denial of values, and tried to show how, in logic, such denial stultifies itself. You cannot, for instance, deny the absoluteness of truth as Huxley does—for example, 'No psychological experience' (that is to say, no conviction, no belief, no idea) 'is "truer", so far as we are concerned, than any other. . . . Science is no "truer" than common sense or lunacy, than art or religion. . . . For, even if one should correspond more closely to things in themselves as perceived by some hypothetical non-human being, it would be impossible for us to discover which it was'— you cannot, I say, make these denials without invalidating your own statement of your case. For, if there is no such thing as truth, it cannot be true to say so; if no theory is 'truer' than another, the arguments against absolute truth are no 'truer' than the contrary arguments in its favour. For the present, however, I am concerned not with logical difficulties but with the practical consequences of this denial of absolute values, and more particularly with the effect upon public taste of the denial of the value of beauty.

That Huxley does deny it, that he is as rude to the other Dowagers, Beauty and Goodness, as he is disrespectful to the dowager Truth, is clear enough to any careful reader of his books. Indeed, he is quite warm about the matter. The following passage disavowing and exposing the Absolutes from his celebrated essay on Pascal is typical: 'A similar conjuring trick . . . draws the Good and the Beautiful out of the seething hotch potch of diverse human tastes and sensibilities and interests, deduces Justice from our actual inequalities, and absolute Truth from the necessary . . . relativities of daily life. It is by an exactly similar process that children invent imaginary playthings to amuse their solitudes, and transform a dull, uninteresting piece of wood into a horse, a ship, a railway train—what you will.'

At the same time Mr. Huxley has become, of late years especially, a very hortatory person. Continually he enjoins us to pursue this kind of activity, to eschew that. Rightly in my view, since some things are, indeed, better, better absolutely and in themselves, than others. Moreover, in his role of guide to which things are in fact better, I find him admirable.

Huxley's Value 'Life'. And the excuse he makes for his apparent inconsistency, for giving advice and, I repeat, such excellent advice, when, on his own premises, he has no business to give advice at all, is that we ought to encourage life and that those things are, therefore, good which promote it. For Life—it seems impossible in view of Huxley's reverential attitude to avoid the capital letter; nor does Huxley avoid it—is, it would seem, for Huxley a value; Life *tout court*. He is, he tells us in this same essay on Pascal, 'a worshipper of life, who accepts all the conflicting facts of human existence'. And the gospel of the Life-accepter is that we should live to the full extent of *all* our various faculties and capacities; we should develop *every* side of our nature, realize *all* that we have it in us to be. The Greek ethic in this connection is praised at the expense of the Christian. To starve one side of our selves in the interests of another, the flesh, for example in order to refine the spirit, the appetites in order to sharpen the mind, is an offence against Life: 'To live', we are told, 'the soul must be in intimate contact with the world, must assimilate it through all the channels of sense and desire, thought and feeling which nature has provided for the purpose.'

As with practice, so with theory. Not only is the gospel of Life the gospel to live by, but the fullest, the best, the most Life-promoting answers to the questions of philosophy are the truest. 'The best answers', Huxley concludes, to the problems of ethics and religion, 'are those which permit the answerer to live most fully.' And, if we ask why this variegated Life, this ballet of all the faculties, this chorus of all the talents, is to be commended, the answer is given in an essay 'One and Many' by a direct judgment of value. 'I am assuming', says Huxley, 'it is an act of faith—that more and intenser life is preferable to less and feebler life.' Life, in fact, is the standard of value, the goal of existence, the meaning of the universe. Life, in short, is divine: 'God for our human purposes', Huxley concludes, 'is simply Life.'

Huxley's 'Life' compared with J. S. Mill's 'Pleasure'. Now this really will not do. It will not do in the first place,

because to reverence Life as such is to shut one's eyes to
the most obvious distinctions of quality. Worshipping
Life as such, Huxley is guilty of the same blunder as
J. S. Mill when, informing us that pleasure alone was
desirable, Mill was forced by the plain facts of experience to make distinctions between qualities of pleasure.
Pleasure alone is the good, said Mill, dutifully echoing
his father, James Mill and Jeremy Bentham. Are all
pleasures, then, we want to know, of equal worth, provided they be of equal amount? Is 'push-pin' really as
good as poetry? Bentham had answered that it was; but
the answer was too much for Mill's common sense. Mill
was a cultivated man of wide interests and generous
sensibilities; he simply could not subscribe to the view
that the pleasures of a pig were as much worth having as
those of a Socrates, merely because their quantity was
the same. And so he concedes: 'Of two pleasures . . . if
one is, by those who are competently acquainted with
both, placed so far above the other that they prefer it,
*even though knowing it to be attended with a greater amount of
discomfort,* and they would not resign it for any quantity
of the other pleasure which their nature is capable of,
we are justified in ascribing to the preferred enjoyment
a superiority in quality so far outweighing quantity, as
to render it in comparison of small account.' 'It is better', he concludes, 'to be a human being dissatisfied
than a pig satisfied.' But the concession virtually des-
troys the position. For, if a smaller quantity of 'higher'
pleasure is to be preferred to a larger quantity of lower,
this can only be because something other than pleasure

is admitted to be desirable, namely its *height*. Now 'higher' pleasure cannot be equated simply with more pleasure, or more intense pleasure, because, if it were, a smaller quantity of 'higher' pleasure would not in fact be a smaller quantity at all; it would simply be *more* pleasure quantitatively. 'Higher' pleasure must, therefore, mean pleasure plus something else which is other than pleasure, but which is also recognized as desirable, and the view that pleasure alone is desirable must be abandoned.

As with Mill's pleasure, so with Huxley's Life. There are, it is obvious, different kinds of life, different kinds and different qualities. The quality of life of the amœba or of the polyp, for example, seems to me to be not only different from a man's but—and I hope that the confession will not set the reader against me on the score of complacency—inferior. It is less vivid, less rich in sensation, less capable of the appreciation of Chartres Cathedral, of the music of Bach or the line of a Sussex down. Yet I have no reason to suppose that the polyp is any less alive than I am. So far as quantity is concerned, our respective degrees of livingness are, I see no reason to doubt, equal. Even among human beings some lives, I should venture to say, are less valuable than others, that of Torquemada than that of Michelangelo, that of Jack the Ripper than that of Mozart.

Life as such not a Good. Life, indeed, as such cannot, it seems to me, be acclaimed a good, merely because it is life. Indiscriminate increase of population beyond the capacity of the country to feed it is, I should say, a definite evil; so is indiscriminate increase of many kinds of bacteria and even quite a moderate increase of cancer cells. Life carries within itself not only ugliness, disease and pain, but the seeds of all that is vicious and hideous in human conduct. It is life that produces cruelty, torture, malice, treachery and rape.

But, if some lives are superior to others, if, to adapt Mill, reading 'life' for 'pleasure', one way of life 'is, by those who are competently acquainted with both, placed so far above the others, that they prefer it, even though knowing it to be attended by' a smaller amount of vitality, 'then we are justified in ascribing to the preferred' life 'a superiority in quality so far outweighing quantity as to render it in comparison of small account'. And in making this obvious concession to common sense, we are forced to give up the simplicity of the original position that all life is equally a good, as Mill was forced to give up the simplicity of the original position that all pleasure is equally a good. For if some lives are to be preferred to others which, being equally full, equally vital, are nevertheless deficient in respect of some quality which causes men to find the former preferable, then some things are valuable besides life.

The conclusion, inescapable in logic, is demanded by the most cursory consideration of acknowledged human valuations. Huxley is completely unable to maintain his position that all kinds of existence are equally valuable provided they be equally 'lively'; with the best will in the world he simply cannot keep it up. Not only, having disavowed value, does he, as we have seen, make a direct judgment of absolute value, the absolute value of Life; he goes on to imply others. At the beginning of his essay on Pascal he provisionally accepts Pascal's classification of the universe into three categories, 'mind, matter and, finally, charity, grace, the supernatural, God or whatever other name you care to bestow on the third of the Pascalian orders'. Admittedly, he goes on to warn us against giving actuality to what are after all only abstractions made by the human intellect. But whatever kind of reality attaches to one order, matter for example, attaches also, he argues, to 'charity, grace, the supernatural'. These, he affirms, are real in precisely the same sense as that in which matter is real. Now Huxley does not in practice trouble to deny the existence of matter, however solipsistic his theory. And in practice he is no less hospitably disposed to the third realm of 'charity, grace, the supernatural', which I now propose to call the realm of value. In fact he persistently and most handsomely recognizes it.

The Cult of 'Lowbrowism'. He has, for example, an admirable essay on the modern cult of 'Lowbrowism'. In 'Foreheads Villainously Low' he discusses the contemporary acceptance, the almost defiant acceptance of 'lowness' in art and life; the shamefaced disavowal of the beautiful and noble. He has, for example, detected Ernest Hemingway in *A Farewell to Arms* suffering himself to speak for a moment of 'the bitter nail holes of Mantegna's Christ', and then shamefacedly passing on

I. Value in the Modern World

'to speak once more of Lower Things'. It is just as if, Huxley comments, Mrs. Gaskell 'had somehow been betrayed into mentioning a water-closet'.

Why this modern fear of culture, or rather this deliberate cult of the low? Huxley has an ingenious explanation. It is because the 'highbrow' is a bad consumer. To sit quietly in one's room with a book, to play Bach on the piano, to wander for a day alone in the country, to give oneself to the enjoyment of 'a green thought in a green shade', does not involve one in consumption, the consumption that is of material goods. Or one consumes very little. Motoring and drinking, going to the races or to football matches, attending the cinema or the theatre, acquiring objects of utility or adornment, one gives employment, contributes to profits, keeps the wheels of industry turning. Contrast the pursuits of the highbrow. The highbrow is emphatically a man with whom advertisement has not succeeded. For my part, I have only to see a commodity advertised to abstain from buying it. Annoyed that the thing should be so blatantly thrust upon my attention, I tell myself that the money which might have gone into making it good has gone, at least in part, into telling me that it is good, when it is not. I know that this argument is economically fallacious; nevertheless, I continue to employ it to justify myself in resisting appeals to buy toothpastes and cigarettes, whenever they are made to me. In pursuance of this policy I have smoked the same tobacco for twenty years, I ring the changes upon a couple of suits until they drop to pieces with age, and dispense with razors altogether

by growing a beard. No doubt I am an extreme example
of the highbrow's advertisement phobia; but there are
plenty like me. The highbrow, then, is a bad consumer,
and to be a bad consumer is to be a bad citizen.

Hence, says Huxley, the modern deliberate cult of
'lowbrowism'; hence the modern disparagement of
values and their resultant lowering.

Huxley the 'Arch-Highbrow'. The explanation, as I say,
is ingenious, but it really will not do. What right, for
example, has Huxley to talk of 'lower values', if all
values are subjective? Yet, when he wishes to castigate
modern civilization, he does talk of them and continuously. Continuously in his essays he passes judgments
which imply that some things are really *better* than
others, better and not merely more vital. Huxley, indeed, is 'the arch-highbrow of modern times'. It is thus
that Low presents him in his *New Statesman* cartoon; it is
thus that the *New Statesman* writer describes him. Not
only is he a highbrow, he is a highbrow more complete
than any age has yet produced, since no age, as the *New
Statesman* writer justly points out, has offered so great a
variety of interests to a detached intelligence. His works
are notable, not because of the solidity and life-likeness
of his characters, but because of the brilliance of their
conversation; not because of the ingenuity of the plots
which he has constructed, but because of the luminous
intelligence of the mind that pervades them. It is in the
dry light of this intelligence that his works are continuously bathed. It is not only upon the sciences that

I. Value in the Modern World

Huxley levies toll for his material, although he knows more about science than any living novelist, but upon history, art, religion, philosophy. He is *par excellence* the detached, cultured intellectual, delighting in what is noble and beautiful, hating what is vulgar and base.

Listen to him, for example, at a 'talkie'. With what a spate of withering invective he castigates the hogwash, the 'not even fresh hogwash. Rancid hogwash, decaying hogwash' of 'yearning Mammy' sentiment, and exhibits for our repulsion 'those mournfully sagging, seasickishly undulating melodies of mother-love and nostalgia and yammering amorousness and clotted sensuality which have been the characteristically Jewish contributions to modern, popular music'. Listen to him again describing the revolution which will finally terminate our civilization, a revolution born not of poverty but of plenty, when mankind, furnished with comfort and a competence on three or four hours machine-minding a day, seeks despairingly for the means of diverting its intolerably protracted leisure. The life that ensues, a life in which 'ready-made creation-saving amusements spread an ever intenser boredom through ever wider spheres', will, he prophesies, be 'pointless and intolerable', how 'pointless' and how 'intolerable' he has striven with praiseworthy success in *Brave New World* to show us.

Entry of Values by the Back Door. But to say of a life that it lacks point and significance, is to say nothing more or less than that it lacks values. For what after all is the matter with *Brave New World*? It has been deliberately bowdlerized of values. It is a world which has been suggested to Huxley by the spectacle of American civilization before the economic flood, a civilization which he deplores with the plaintive observation, 'America has twenty-five million motor cars but almost no original art.' Why does he deplore it? Because, he tells us, of its 'depressing effects on those human activities hitherto regarded as the most *valuable*' (my italics).

Huxley on Music. That Huxley is in truth intensely sensitive to values, and more particularly to the value we call beauty, nobody who has read him on the subject of music can doubt. That admirable passage at the beginning of *Point Counterpoint* where Lord Tantamount abandons his laboratory and appears shamefacedly among his guests drawn by the strains of Bach's suite in B Minor for flute and strings, is conclusive evidence of the awareness by his creator not only of the 'point' of things, but of the significance of the part played by beauty in giving them 'point'. Not only is Huxley intensely sensitive to values when he finds them, he can draw a terrifying picture of the man who can find nothing else. Spandrell, at the end of the same book, playing the Adagio Molto of the Beethoven A Minor quartet, Opus 132, prior to committing suicide, and finding in it apparently a complete answer to the riddle of the universe—it was, says Huxley, commenting on the effect produced by the music at the performance of the play based on the book, it was 'as though a god had really and visibly descended, awful and yet reassuring,

mysteriously wrapped in the peace that passes all understanding, divinely beautiful'—is a frightful warning
against being so perceptive of significance, so drunk
with value, that one can no longer tolerate a world
which contains so little of it. (It is a pity, I cannot help
thinking, that Huxley invoked a posthumous Beethoven
quartet to illustrate his point. Beethoven does *not* convey
the quiet assurance of a perfectly understood universe.
What he is all the time saying is 'Here at last I am telling
you the true, the final answer to things, *if* you could
only understand me; here at last are the real cosmic
goods, *if* I could only "put them across".' But you don't
understand him, and he does not 'put them across'. Now
Schubert, writing a year later, just seven weeks before
his death, in the same vein, did manage to be comprehensible about the cosmos, did 'put it across'. Take,
for instance, the Andante Sostenuto of the B Flat
sonata. Here is not something which would be ineffable,
did one but understand it. One *does* understand it, and
it *is* ineffable. And there is not that sense of sweat and
strain, that creaking of the machinery which in Beethoven. . . . However, I perceive that I am mounting a
hobbyhorse.)

Use of Inadmissible Expressions. Nor does Huxley in this
vein hesitate to use the most tendentious, the most inadmissible expressions. Music, he tells us, is 'divinely
beautiful', and proceeds to speak[1] of the 'intuition of
beauty' as something which 'profoundly significant, can

[1] In 'The Rest is Silence', an Essay in *Music at Night*.

only be experienced not expressed'. As for the language which he employs in describing the *Benedictus* in Beethoven's *Missa Solemnis* in the title essay of the volume,[1] it is nothing short of scandalous. We hear of 'the blessedness that is at the heart of things', of the power of great art to express this 'blessedness'. We read that 'the substance of a work of art is inseparable from its form', and of 'the eloquence of pure form'. We learn that the 'truth and the beauty' of works of art are 'two and yet, mysteriously, one', and are warned that we cannot isolate 'the truth contained in a piece of music; for it is a beauty truth and inseparable from its partner'.

Now what sort of language is this for a man who owns no values but that of vitality? Beautiful music does not always and necessarily increase vitality—it killed Spandrell—and, even when it does, it is not for that reason that we value it. The first movement of Bach's violin concerto in E Flat, for example, is full of life. Moreover, it heightens the vitality of those who hear it. The second, slow, reflective, mysteriously lovely, is not vital at all. It carries one, in common parlance, out of this life altogether into another world. Nevertheless, we do not value it either less or more than the first, for the simple reason that vitality has nothing to do with beauty. No, Huxley cannot keep it up; that is to say, he cannot keep values out. He may refuse to recognize the dowagers officially; he may even kick them down the front door steps; but they will come in by the back.

[1] *Music at Night.*

I. Value in the Modern World

Huxley as a Moralist. And of course he is right; right, not in his official attitude, but in his practical repudiation of it. A sensitive and fastidious man, he cannot abstain from passionately preferring, acutely discriminating. The fact that he cannot intellectually justify his discriminations does not prevent him from making them. Nor could it; for it is impossible for a cultivated man not to acknowledge the existence of that, in virtue of his sensibility to which, he is cultivated. He may, out of mental cussedness, refuse to recognize value in theory; but his whole life is an acknowledgment of it in practice. Huxley is a brilliant writer, an admirable wit, a keen satirist, a good art critic; so much is implied in the title of 'arch-highbrow'. But Huxley is something more than a highbrow, something more, and, from his official standpoint, something worse. He is also a powerful and original moralist with a passion for reforming his kind. He is thoroughly ashamed of this passion, and does his best to disavow it; but there is no mistaking the note which is so frequently sounded in his later works. It is the note of Swift, of Bunyan, of Blake, Emerson, J. A. Kensit and Bernard Shaw, the authentic note of the moral reformer to whom it is so intolerable to see people muddling their thoughts and mismanaging their lives, that he simply cannot restrain himself from telling them how to think better and behave more sensibly.

As moral reformer no less than as 'highbrow' moralist Huxley has done work of the highest importance. He has enriched the mind and cleansed the morals of our generation. He has opened its eyes to the futility of cleverness without ideals, and 'debunked' the delights of the 'good time'. Also he has written some very lovely prose.

Huxley, then, is a man pre-eminently aware of value; he knows goodness, and wishes to see it actualized in the lives of men. Hence his moral earnestness. He is sensitive to beauty, and pays tribute to it wherever he finds it. Hence his preoccupation with art and music; hence the loveliness of such an essay as *Music at Night*. But though he is sensitive to value and pays tribute to it in his works, to goodness in his didactic essays and to beauty in his poems and art criticism, it would be absurd to say that Huxley is a very vital man, taking the word 'vital' in its strict and literal sense to imply rich and abounding life. On the contrary he is a man who deliberately chooses to live a quiet and secluded life. He does not even inhabit his own country; he withdraws himself to the Continent. He takes no part in public affairs, and seems far too impatient of the follies and stupidities of his fellows to be able to co-operate with them. He is physically far from robust, is not given to playing games and by his own admission abhors the pursuits of 'hearties'. No, Huxley is not a supremely vital man.

Romantic Admiration of Life. Hence, perhaps, his romantic admiration for vitality. Just as at the end of the last century physically weak men like Henley and Stevenson, living at the close of an era of prolonged peace, indulged in a romantic admiration for violent action—listen for example to that fool Ruskin telling us

I. Value in the Modern World

in *The Crown of Wild Olive* that 'war is the foundation of all the high virtues and faculties of man'—so Huxley, it may be, delights to laud the vitality which he is morbidly conscious of not possessing.

Judged by his own standard of vitality as the sole and exclusive criterion of value, Huxley is, I fear, a very worthless person. He does not employ his physical faculties at full stretch; he does not live the life of the passions and the senses; his actions are not vigorous or robust. He is not close to the heart of nature, nor does he rub shoulders with the world, 'assimilating it through all the channels of sense and desire, thought and feeling which nature has provided for the purpose'. I doubt even whether he makes hearty meals. Compared, for example, with Adolf Hitler, Falstaff, Torquemada, Cobbett, or even Casanova is he very little alive. And yet, I maintain, that he is a man of very great value indeed. And the measure of his value is the measure of his error. This romantic admiration of life as such is, as I have already pointed out, palpable nonsense. Much life is horrible and ought not to be at all. Life produced the Inquisition, the lynching of negroes and the Slave Trade; it proliferates into cancers; Goering is excessively alive. . . .

As a child my æsthetic taste was execrable; moreover, it remained execrable until an unusually late period. But, bad as it was, it was very vivid, particularly so in music. I hummed, sang and whistled the popular songs of the day with gusto, dissolved into delicious woefulness over sentimental ballads, and melted to the erotic rhythms of the Viennese Waltzes to which young men's fancies then turned. The Chocolate Soldier Waltz seemed to me the high-water mark of musical composition, and I considered a short popular piece called 'In the Shadows' one of the prettiest things ever written. Looking back I have no doubt at all about the degree of my liking for these things. I absorbed them voraciously, and obtained the very greatest pleasure from their assimilation. As with music, so with food. There were certain simple comestibles to which as a child I was particularly partial, treacle, for instance, or syrup of figs, from which I should now recoil with horror; while bread and dripping, which I still view with respect, seemed to me at the time almost divine in its flavour.

To say that these tastes of mine were not vital, not fully alive, is nonsense. To say that they were good is equally nonsense. Good, therefore, is not to be equated with vital. Why then should the attempt, in spite of all the evidence to the contrary, to equate them be made? And why in particular should it be made with such tiresome frequency by this generation? Why, in fact, the cult of deliberate 'lowbrowism' which Huxley so rightly ridicules, yet which his refusal to admit absolute values implicitly endorses?

The Snobbery of Anti-Culture. As to the fact, there can, I think, be no reasonable doubt. Whereas in the Victorian age a taste for the highest and best was considered so important that people, who were unable to distinguish between Mendelssohn and Beethoven, talked learnedly of diminished sevenths and rapturously of the genius of the great composers, while ladies who were unable to understand half a dozen sentences of *One of Our Conquerors* were eager to include in their small talk an advance announcement of Mr. Meredith's new novel, to-day the avowal of a taste for Beethoven is considered embarrassing, for Meredith absurd, while cultivated and intelligent persons, concealing their knowledge of the arts, talk learnedly about the averages of cricket professionals and the predilections of prizefighters. The tides of culture snobbery have set in the opposite direction, and while few moderns would be willing to confess to a taste for Bach and Wordsworth, they would willingly avow their admiration for *Razzle* and Jack Hylton's band.

Nothing is more remarkable in this connection than the *volte-face* which in the space of a few years can be seen to occur in the taste of contemporary young women. Educated at their girls' schools to love the highest when they see it, they leave at the age of seventeen or eighteen with tastes of great elevation and refinement. They read Keats and Shakespeare, put prints of Botticelli and Michelangelo on the walls of their rooms, and clamour to be taken to hear Schnabel, compared with whose rendering of Beethoven that of no other pianist is, they aver, endurable. Within a couple of years the contemporary young woman, left to her own devices, has discarded her school culture with as little compunction as she discards her school chapel and her school clothes. Jazz instead of music, Edgar Wallace instead of literature and Greta Garbo registering amorous ecstasy on the 'talkies' replace those earlier schoolgirl loves, Chopin and Puccini, Browning and Rossetti, Francis Thompson and Ruskin and Stevenson. Piano playing is dropped, Michelangelo and Botticelli disappear from the walls, and a detective story or a 'blood' by Sapper or Wren does duty for reading. If by any chance the young woman's development is sufficiently retarded to enable her to retain her taste for great literature and high thoughts, she is careful to let no word which might betray her secret indulgences pass her lips.

Glance at the Modern Scene. The phenomenon of school-girls jettisoning their gods is only one expression of a deliberate cult of childishness in thought and expression, in music, morals and art. We talk in words of one syllable from a deliberately limited vocabulary, produce deliberately neo-primitive pictures and statues, croon nigger songs without tune or sense, as we gently direct one another to and fro in dances which, needing neither skill nor vitality, are equally lacking in gusto and in grace. We tear over the earth's surface along roads of brick-box straightness, past houses of brick-box dimensions, in order to arrive in record time at places in which we shall do nothing at all. Our novels are concerned with the activities, physiological and psychological, of those parts of our organism which we share with animals, children and savages, and devote the often not inconsiderable intelligences of their authors to representing human beings as creatures devoid of intelligence, whose actions are motivated from the solar plexus rather than from the brain.

I have known for years the son of one of the leading literary figures of the Edwardian literary world. He was brought up in an atmosphere impregnated with culture. At his earliest family meals he met its living exponents. The talk was all of Meredith and Hardy, of Wilde, Patmore and Pater, of Francis Thompson and of that blaspheming poet James Thomson, B.V. Arrived at man's estate my friend ruthlessly discarded culture and started to play ball games. With the taste of the artist he appraises tennis shots and cricket strokes; he applauds bruisers with the fervour of the poet; with the patience of the mathematician he memorizes cricket averages, and with all the force of his being he clamorously backs the Arsenal. He is a symptom, an extreme symptom, of the 'lowbrowism' of the age, an age which, inheriting Chartres Cathedral, asserts itself by confronting it with aeroplane sheds.

To me there is something essentially repulsive in a comparatively mature civilization playing with the toys of immaturity, when it knows better; there is something horrible in the lacklustre enjoyments of the modern 'good time', the negroid music, the gloomy dances, the deliberately stupid conversation, the shame of intelligence. Adult minds cannot think childishly and also think spontaneously; grown men cannot pursue the tastes of schoolboys with schoolboys' abandon.

Am I here merely voicing a personal dislike, or has my repulsion some objective basis in an intrinsic repulsive-ness in that which provokes it? Is my regret for the culture of the past merely a middle-aged man's nostalgia for his own childhood, or is there really cause for disquietude in the 'lowbrowism' of the age? In a word, do beauty and truth really matter, or is it just a private whim of my own to think that they do? These questions which raise an old controversy in a new form demand a chapter to themselves.

Chapter III

Defence of Value—II. Beauty

★

The 'Symposium'. Plato's *Symposium* contains a celebrated account of the journey of the soul in search of beauty. Beauty, which Plato conceives as an immaterial Form, is apprehended after a process of æsthetic development, which, beginning with the appreciation of the beauty of single beautiful objects and persons, comes to recognize the common quality of beauty which distinguishes them as members of a class and so to appreciate classes of beautiful objects and persons, proceeds to the appreciation of abstract beauty in laws and morals, then to the sciences and a realization of the beauty of Science, and so at last reaches a knowledge of the Form itself.[1]

It is interesting to notice that the kind of knowledge which we call scientific immediately precedes the knowledge of beauty. It is the scientist who occupies the stage immediately below that of the artist, the artist, that is, conceived not as executant but as seer. The statement, which sounds a little startling to modern ears—we know

[1] Plato. *Symposium*, 210, 211.

our scientists, and, whatever they do or do not do, they do not contemplate the Form of Beauty, not, at least, obtrusively—is mitigated by the consideration that for Plato scientific knowledge meant pre-eminently mathematical knowledge. The mathematician, then, is the person whose insight seemed to Plato most closely to approximate to that of the seer.

The Training of the Mind to know Beauty. A hint dropped in the *Republic* may help to throw light on Plato's meaning. We are here told that the proper education of the mind for a knowledge of the Forms is a training in the exact sciences of measuring, weighing and counting, namely, the Theories of Number, Geometry, Stereometry and Astronomy.[1] The mind, in other words, is to be trained in precision; it must observe accurately and reason correctly. The apprehension of the Form is, it seems, not lightly to be achieved, nor, indeed, is it possible except to minds which have been prepared by hard and continuous exercise in abstract intellectual pursuits. Clive Bell, in his book *Art*, endorses this hint of Plato's as to the affinity between beauty and mathematics. The distinguishing characteristic of great art, he points out, is that in the moment of contemplation, we are completely shut off from the world of human interests: 'Our anticipations and memories are arrested; we are lifted above the stream of life. The pure mathematician rapt in his studies knows a state of mind which I take to be similar, if not identical. He feels an emotion

[1] Plato. *Republic*, 525-8.

95

II. Beauty

for his speculations which arises from no perceived relation between them and the lives of men, but springs, inhuman or superhuman, from the heart of an abstract science. I sometimes wonder whether the appreciators of art and of mathematical solutions are not even more closely allied. Before we feel an æsthetic emotion for a combination of forms, do we not perceive intellectually the rightness and necessity of the combination?'

To return to Plato. The apprehension of the Form itself is, in the *Symposium*, described in the language of a mystical vision; the Form will, we are told, 'shine forth'. But the vision, though conditioned by, is logically divorced from the strictly intellectual process which leads up to it.

The hint of the *Symposium* is confirmed by the testimony of subsequent writers. That meditation and contemplation are the necessary preliminaries to the mystical vision, and that meditation and contemplation involve not merely or always a purely receptive state of intellectual passivity, there is ample evidence in the literature of mysticism. Some writers go further and insist upon the need for hard mental discipline and training.

The Leap of the Mind from Knowledge to Vision. There also seems to be good evidence for the *abruptness* of the transition from one level of apprehension to another. Between the worlds of becoming and of being there was fixed for Plato a definite gulf, a gulf which the mind must leap to obtain its vision of Beauty. There is a leap

96

too from any one stage of the leading-up process to the next, from the apprehension of a thing as an object useful or useless, rare or worthless, to the apprehension of it as what Clive Bell calls significant form, that is, as 'a combination of lines and colours . . . that moves us æsthetically'.

Now this leaping, this mental jump, is, it seems to me, a plain fact of æsthetic experience. You look at a tree on many occasions and notice it only as possible timber, or as an elm, or as dangerous; or you do not notice it at all. Then comes a day when you *suddenly* notice that it is beautiful. And it is the same with a picture; its beauty *suddenly* strikes us.

Consider in this connection one's appreciation of the typical Dutch picture. Apparently a coloured photograph of a simple scene, in which every detail is accurately reproduced—it is one of the most difficult exercises I know to try to state in what respect a Vermeer differs from a coloured photograph—the picture is invested with a significance which the scene itself lacks. Or lacks for most people! For Vermeer, I suppose, differs from most people in being able to see in the scene the significance which we cannot observe save in the picture. What he has done is to drag significance from the irrelevant setting in which it lurked, and throw it into high relief. He does not create beauty; he is the midwife who brings to birth the beauty that is latent in things.

The Need for Practice. The point, however, which I

II. Beauty

wish chiefly to bring out in Plato's account is the insistence upon the need for practice. It is practice which, at every stage of the process, paves the way for the next, preparing the mind for the jumps which it must make, if its vision of the universe is to be so deepened and enlarged that it may discern beauty. And practice has this effect partly because the objects apprehended at each stage possess the property of directing the mind's attention to the next. Not only is it the function of education to wheel the soul 'round from the perishing world' to 'the contemplation of the real world and the brightest part thereof',[1] but the visible world itself possesses the power of 'turning the eye of the soul' towards the intelligible.

The process of jumping by the mind from one level of apprehension to another, which at first sight seems sufficiently mysterious when it occurs in the æsthetic realm, is accepted without comment in the physical. I say 'the mind', although, when it is the physical organism that learns a new trick, the credit for it should perhaps go to the body that performs it. Every fresh acquisition of bodily skill and accomplishment is achieved as the result of hard and unremitting effort. It is the fruit of continual practice which for long seems to bring no improvement. To remember how we learned to ride a bicycle, or to 'do' an outside edge, is to remember periods of seemingly hopeless endeavour, in which only the desire to perform the apparent miracle which others wrought with such assurance, kept us going. And

[1] Plato. *Republic*, vii, 518.

the acquisition, when it was made, came all at once; one was making—was one not?—those same ineffective efforts which one had always made, when suddenly to one's immense surprise they succeeded. They succeeded, and one 'did it'. And 'did it', whatever 'it' was, from the first almost perfectly. The body, in fact—or was it the mind?—had made a jump to a new level of accomplishment, achieving a balance or a movement which was previously utterly beyond its compass.

The Level of Insight not Retained. And as with the mind, so too with the body, the jump, although the result of hard practice and continuous effort, is itself effortless. But, unlike the mind, the body, having made its achievement, retains it. One cannot forget to swim, although one can quickly lose the capacity to apprehend beauty.

The difference is as significant as it is lamentable. It is significant in its bearing upon the questions with which the last chapter concluded. What, I asked, is the reason for the deliberate contempt of beauty, for the deliberate distrust of intelligence, which is so characteristic of our age? And the answer that immediately suggests itself is the ease, the distressing ease with which 'taste' can be lost. Good taste, which is a part of what I mean by 'the capacity to apprehend beauty', is, it is obvious, not instinctive in our species; it is something acquired. Children's taste, in literature crude, is in music execrable. Children do not, except when admonished thereto by adults, respond to nature, appreciate sonnets, or

love the highest when they see it. Broadly speaking, it is
not until puberty is reached that the æsthetic sense can
be said to exist. Even then it must be trained, practised
and disciplined, if it is not to run riot in the lush jungle
of the 'talkies', the 'crooners' and the best sellers which
are the distinctive contribution of our age to art.

Built up with difficulty, maintained by constant exercise, good taste is lost with fatal facility. When we are
ill, in pain, or marooned on desert islands, it is our
tastes for Bach and Shakespeare which are the first to
fall away from us. It is not true that man in affliction
can listen to music, or that man in the wilderness can
read poetry.

The Function of Environment. The activity of the æsthetic
sense, in apprehending and appreciating beauty, can, it is
obvious, only function where there are peace of mind
and freedom from bodily hardship. It also requires an
appropriate environment. It seems to me that Plato's
insistence on this point in the early books of the *Republic*
has never been treated with the respect it deserves. That
the body can only function properly, can only grow to
its full stature in an environment of light, space and air,
suitably clad, adequately and appropriately fed, that the
body, in fact, reflects its environment is accepted, and
we feel no surprise when we learn that the infant mortality rate in a South Wales colliery district should be
more than a third higher than it is in Bournemouth or
Hampstead, and nearly a tenth higher than it was before the slump. But that what is true of the body should

be true also of the mind, spirit, soul, call it what you will: that the soul too will reflect its environment, we seem not to realize. At any rate the realization, if it exists, does not affect our practice.

Yet it is precisely this upon which Plato insists, insists so strongly that he makes it the keystone of his educational system. Bring up a human being in beautiful surroundings, accustom him to harmonious forms and musical sounds, to gracious manners and dignified intercourse, and his soul will become harmonious, graceful, beautiful. He will have, in a word, good taste. Bring him up in a mean environment of factories, slums or villas, accustom him to the sound of loud voices, to the sight of ugly forms, and teach him to equate beauty with vulgar and ostentatious ornamentation, and his soul will be mean, vulgar and trivial. He will have, in a word, bad taste.

This is no place to enlarge upon the spate of ugliness and vulgarity, the acres of mean streets and undistinguished houses, with which unrestricted private enterprise, driven by the mania for quick profits covered England in the last century. We can see them for ourselves by merely driving in any direction from the centre of London to its outskirts. The predominant note is not even hideousness, but a monotonous dreariness of bricks and mortar unparalleled, one believes and hopes, in the universe. And it stretches for miles and miles and miles of desolation, not a wen, as Cobbett in his day called it, but a vast malignant growth. What a monument to nineteenth-century civilization it is, this teeming desert of mean houses, ugly shops, ugly houses and mean shops repeating themselves endlessly from Woolwich to Wimbledon, from Purley to Highgate, and from Acton to Wood Green. Is it any wonder that those brought up amid such surroundings should reflect in their tastes and pursuits the environment which has stamped their souls, that they should like trivial books, empty plays and vulgar films, and that they should be so little able to come to terms with nature that their reaction to natural beauty, when they do come into contact with it, should be to fence and to enclose it, to deluge it with litter, to uproot its flowers and carve its trees, spoiling and ravishing it, until they have effectively destroyed the beauty they could not tolerate?

Smells, Noises and Islands of Escape. Or consider the noises of our civilization! We are apt to look back upon the men and women of the Middle Ages with pitying contempt because of their lack of drains. And no doubt their streets and persons smelled very badly. The grand ladies of Elizabeth's time in particular, swathed in voluminous wrappings, lacking cotton underclothes, and sewn up in wool which they changed only at rare intervals, must have outrageously offended the environing air. We have spared our noses at the expense of our ears. The world may not smell to-day as it did four hundred years ago, but never assuredly was it so noisy. Every fresh labour-saving device, every new creation-saving amusement lets loose a fresh flood of ugly sound upon our ears; and, because we make no instinctive de-

mand for beauty in our environment, because we have
grown insensitive to its lack, because, in a word, our
ears are attuned to ugliness, nobody seems very much
to mind.

I am sometimes reproached for spending my holidays
in primitive places; often on islands without civilized
hotels or organized amusements, without drains or
electric light, with muddy paths for their only roads,
from the refuse piled along the sides of which every
shower of rain brings out a varied assortment of steamy
smells. Why, I am asked, do I go so far to seek such un-
savoury places? There is a number of answers to this
question, most of which are not relevant to my present
theme; as, for example, that I share Huxley's horror of
a 'good time', that I regard the amusements and enter-
tainments of the ordinary 'resort' as the most formidable contrivance for inducing mass boredom which the
misplaced ingenuity of mankind has devised, and that
since I find work in the shape of reading and writing
interspersed with daydreaming by streams, in woods or
on high cliffs overlooking the sea, the only form of occupation which I can tolerate in any but the very smallest
doses, I must go somewhere where I can read, write and
daydream undisturbed. And in the places where civilized men and women deliberately amuse themselves,
even more than in the places where they work, these
things are impossible.

But the immediately relevant answer is that on islands
one is reasonably assured of quiet. On those remote fragments of land which lie off the coasts of Cornwall and

II. Beauty

Brittany I am secure from motors, I am reasonably likely to be undisturbed by gramophones, and the wireless has only just begun to penetrate. True, I must read at night by candle light, but then my reading in the morning is not disturbed by a motor or a dynamo making electric light for me to see by at night. As there are no roads, I am spared electric drills, and since the population consists of peasants and fishermen, nobody at present thinks it worth while to croon to them the rhythmic banalities of negroid music. These primitive and unpleasing sounds are considered suitable for the delectation only of civilized persons.

Resorts. Let us suppose that I am so ill advised as to leave my island, and endeavour to divert myself at some place where the civilized gather. Immediately I am exposed to a more varied cacophony of ugly sounds than has hitherto assaulted the eardrums of any race of beings. There are, first, the sounds of labour-saving devices; motor cars and motor horns, vacuum cleaners and electric drills, electric motors and dynamos for making light. In almost every continental resort each hotel has its own separate plant for manufacturing light. Early in the morning the monotonous beat of the motor or the whirr of the dynamo makes itself heard. Relentlessly it continues hour after hour, until nerves are frayed, good temper gone, and brains so dissipated that hours of tranquillity are required for their recall. Meanwhile men saw, hammer, knock and nail; carpets are beaten, furniture repaired, awnings put up or taken down. Worse, much worse, are the sounds of pleasure; of radio and gramophone and Wurlitzer organ. From the middle of the day onwards the sounds of mechanical music makers begin to pervade the atmosphere. By nightfall the outraged air is one vast vibration of cacophonous crooning. Silence, peace and tranquillity, these things have gone from the civilized world no less than the solitude in which they may be enjoyed; gone so completely, that many are unaware that they ever existed. Can we suppose that a soul brought up in such an environment will not take colour from its surroundings, colour of sound as well as of sight, and become insensitive and coarse in proportion as its channels, the senses, convey to it for its sustenance not only ugly sights but also ugly noises? Souls that do not reflect beauty will not be moved to create it or to demand it; should it be presented to them, they will not notice that it is there.

Musical Taste. In the Elizabethan and Jacobean ages England produced a school of musicians. Purcell and Byrd, Locke, Gibbons and Lawes are, indeed, among the great musicians of the world. Their music is exceedingly difficult, so difficult that it is only when we moderns have been long coached by the careful performances of the Dolmetsch family that our ears are opened and we can hear. It is also difficult to play. Yet, we are assured, the guests at an average Jacobean party played it as a normal part of their after-dinner entertainment. It was as natural for them to play good music for themselves as it is for us to listen to bad music brayed for us by a gramophone.

II. Beauty

And fundamentally it is our environment that has disabled us from appreciating the good. In the nineteenth century, when musical appreciation in England sank to its lowest ebb, men could not listen even to Bach. It was more than an organist's place was worth to announce a Bach prelude or fugue for his voluntary; if he introduced Bach's music, it had to be done surreptitiously. To-day, thanks to the B.B.C. and Sir Henry Wood, our taste has improved, and although Wagner still draws his now rather elderly hundreds to the Queen's Hall, the Bach nights are the most popular at the proms. Good taste then is, at least in part, born of environment. Change the environment, as war changes it or revolution, change it by increasingly applying science to productive processes—the change from the art and taste of the late eighteenth to those of the mid-nineteenth century seems to have been mainly due to the changes in modes of production introduced by the Industrial Revolution—and, as the Russian experiment has shown, you can produce incalculable effects upon the taste of those who live in it, so that, while one generation will love and demand beauty, another can be happy only with ornament. It is only precariously that the mind of man maintains itself at the level at which it is capable of æsthetic appreciation; disturb the environment, and it can slip back to a lower rung of the ladder of taste with a dismaying ease.

The Conditions for the Production of Great Art. If a jump is involved in the appreciation of beauty, it is involved no less in its creation, or rather, as I should prefer to say, in its discovery[1]. In art, as in science, the environment most favourable for the production of work of the highest order is that of the school, the workshop, the laboratory, the studio or the coterie. It is, in a word, a community of fellow craftsmen. Where many are doing good work, there will always be a chance of some doing great work. The Brandenburg Concertos would not have been written, had there been no Bach to write them; but equally they would not have been written, had not a long line of past musicians bequeathed Bach a tradition, and a school of contemporary musicians maintained for him an environment of high general output giving him at once a stimulus, a standard and an atmosphere. Similarly, the quantum theory would not have been announced to the world, unless Planck had made his experiments on the heating of black bodies; but Planck would never have made his experiments, would never, indeed, have had his attention drawn to the possibilities of black bodies at all, if it had not been for the high standard of attainment of the German school of physicists among whom he lived, with whom he worked, from whom, it might almost be said, he derived his being. Partly, no doubt, the reason for this excellence of achievement lies in the value to the creative worker of continuous and informed criticism. Constant interchange of ideas and reciprocal criticism of results not only ensure the maintenance of a reasonably

[1] See Chapter VIII, especially pages 229, 230, 233 for a defence of this expression.

II. Beauty

high level of output; they prevent the excesses into which the creative artist working in solitude and thrown helpless upon his own taste and judgment is only too liable to fall. More important perhaps than this negative check, is the fact that a community or school of competent men maintaining a high general standard of work provides a propitious environment for that jumping of the spirit to new levels of conscious awareness which is the occasion of great art.

The distinctive quality of the great artist is his capacity for becoming aware for the first time of something that has hitherto been overlooked. This quality, too, I would submit,[1] is the outstanding characteristic of the great philosopher, the great scientist and the great mathematician. Whatever we term this 'something'—significant relations of form and colour, significant combinations of sound in music or of symbols in mathematics, the sudden synthesis of hitherto uncoordinated ideas in science or philosophy—its discernment on the part of the creative artist involves and is conditioned by a jump to a new level of conscious apprehension. I say 'creative', and yet the activity involved is more properly one of discovering than of creating. It is analogous to the activity of a map reader who by virtue of a superior clarity of vision discerns, let us say, a track marked on an old map which has hitherto escaped notice.

[1] I have tried to give reasons for this view in *Philosophical Aspects of Modern Science*, Chapters X and XI. (Allen and Unwin.)

The 'Jump' a Psychological Experience

The 'Jump' a Psychological Experience. This activity of
'jumping' on the part of the mind or, rather, the character of the universe to which it points, namely, that its
contents are revealed as a hierarchy of levels or orders
apprehended by different levels of conscious awareness,
demands, I think, metaphysical interpretation. This I
have attempted elsewhere.[1] Here, since psychological
facts are the only kind of facts of which Huxley is prepared to take account, I must content myself with pointing out that the 'jumping' on the part of the æsthetic and
intellectual consciousness is a recognizable fact of our
psychological experience. Granted that it is, I proceed
to ask whether it does not involve just that conception
of value and of orders of value in the universe which
Huxley, in his capacity of representative of modern
thought, denies.

If the answer be simply that there is no such 'jump',
or, if the 'jump' be admitted, that it points to nothing of
the kind, I do not see how the denial can be met. If a
man says there is no such thing as toothache, I do not
see how I can prove to him that there is. I can assure
him that I have it, but I cannot communicate my
assurance to him. Psychological facts, as Huxley himself
when he writes of the mystics points out, are strictly in-
communicable. At this point, then, we reach the limits
of argument. But only at this point. It is only if we insist
on remaining within the sphere of strictly personal experience, that we must admit to having reached an

[1] See my *Matter, Life and Value*, Chapters VI, VIII, and IX.
(Oxford University Press.)

impasse. But there are other spheres; that of philosophy
for instance. For, if Huxley does deny the 'jump', or,
while admitting it, denies that it points to value in the
universe, we are entitled to probe deeper and to enquire
why he denies it. He does not, I understand, deny the
psychological fact which is the experience of apprehending the toothache. Why, then, does he deny the experience which is the apprehension of a value?

Transition to Philosophy. The answer is, I think, because of his general philosophical position, a position
which, while permitting him to concede that there are
teeth which do in their own right ache, requires him to
deny that there are pictures which are in their own right
beautiful and sounds which are in their own right harmonious. He may not call this position of his philosophical. In fact, it is, as we shall see, part of his philosophy to deny that a philosophical position can be anything more than the rationalization of a set of subjective
preferences and prejudices, to deny, in fact, that philosophy can be fruitful. Nevertheless he *has* a philosophical
position from which his repudiation of absolute values
necessarily follows.

We must, then, proceed to consider what this position
is. Is it, we shall further want to know, plausible? Is it
consistent? Is it exposed to obvious difficulties? Does it
square with known facts? These are questions which
may be legitimately asked of any philosophy. If we see
reason to answer them in the negative, then the consequences which follow on the assumption that the posi-

tion is sound, and only on that assumption, can be set aside. One of these consequences is the denial of the objective reality of value. Here, then, is a legitimate field for discussion; here is a course upon which those who wish to challenge the Huxleyan repudiation, which is also the characteristically modern repudiation, of value, may profitably embark.

But the task is a formidable one. We are, we shall find, committed to a criticism of a whole philosophy of life. It is a philosophy which, in addition to denying the absolute reality of value, denies also the absolute competence of human reason. In the sphere of thought it denies the capacity of the human reason to reach truth, and consequently discards philosophy in favour of science; in that of practice it denies the right or the ability of reason to lay down rules of conduct, and consequently discards principles in favour of experiment.

Author's Programme. Now this philosophy receives, as I have already hinted, its most characteristically modern expression in the writings of Aldous Huxley. We are committed, then, to a critical examination of the characteristic philosophy of Huxley, to a defence of reason in theory and practice, and to a defence of philosophy as a mode of reaching truth. While we may hope to soften the austerity of our undertaking[1] by an occasional glance at some of the consequences, the all too common consequences which follow the contemporary disparagement of reason, our main task as

[1] As in the first chapter.

II. Beauty

avowed defenders of value, reason and philosophy, will be the carrying out of the formidable philosophical programme outlined. Nor will its completion see the end of our defence. For, sensitive to the charge of being merely critical, I propose to add two chapters which will seek to perform the office of construction by outlining in a few pages, and with particular reference to the questions raised in the preceding chapter, the metaphysical view which I have endeavoured to set out at length elsewhere.

These constructive suggestions may at the same time be considered in the light of a continuation at a more fundamental level of my defence of reason and of philosophy. In working them out I shall be led to indicate what is, in my view, the ultimate status of value in the universe, and the ultimate *raison d'être* of those human activities, art and mysticism, which chiefly seek to trap and embody it. This indication will be offered in lieu of that formal defence of value which in the present chapter, as I am only too conscious, I may seem to have shirked.

Chapter IV

Defence of Value—III. Aldous Huxley and the Dowagers

★

Aldous Huxley has written a series of admirable essays[1] which, ostensibly concerned with Pascal, are in effect a disquisition on philosophy. Huxley avows the fact. 'Pascal is really only an excuse and a convenience,' he writes. 'If I choose to write about him, it is because he raises, either by implication in his life, or explicitly in his writings, practically all the major problems of philosophy and conduct.' 'In the margin of' what he calls Pascal's 'guide book', Huxley has 'pencilled a few reflections. This essay', he continues, 'is made up of them. Pascal is only incidentally its subject.' And the disquisition upon philosophy turns out upon examination to be less a disquisition than an assault, an assault of which the object is to show that philosophy, as opposed to science and, presumably, to common sense, is and must of necessity be moonshine. The word is not Huxley's—he is indeed exquisitely polite to philosophy —but I want to convey briefly the upshot of his essay,

[1] Published in the volume of collected essays entitled *Do What You Will*.

and he will forgive a philosopher for using bluntly the words that he has minced.

Huxley's Criticism of Philosophy. The assault, directed against philosophy as a whole, has for its special objective rationalistic philosophy, that is to say, metaphysical systems which claim to be able to discover the fundamental nature of the universe by sheer process of logical reasoning. And what Huxley has to say about them is something like this.

If you want to know what the universe is like, you must go and see; in other words, you must follow the methods of science. Observe facts, correlate them, state your conclusions in the form of scientific laws, and your laws will apply to something. They will give you, that is to say, information about a world external to yourself; they are, to drop into philosophical jargon, objectively valid.

Directly, however, you begin to speculate about the facts that science catalogues, directly you begin to follow out their implications, to reason at large about them, to make inferences from facts about a special department of the universe to the universe as a whole, to infer, for example, what sort of universe it must be in order that the facts in question may occur in it, directly, in a word, you assume the function of the philosopher, then your results are no longer objectively valid; they are merely rationalizations of your subjective needs and wishes. They cease to apply to any world outside yourself; they merely reflect yourself. What the philosopher does, in fact, is not to present us with a picture of the universe, but merely to project the creations of his own intellectual imagination upon its empty canvas.[1] Having projected them, he discovers with a naïve surprise what he has projected, and announces a metaphysical system. The philosopher, in short, is one who fares through the uttermost confines of the universe to find himself.

Thus Descartes is criticized because being a rationalist 'he believed in the reality of his abstractions. Inventing fictions, he imagined that he was revealing the truth'. Nor is it only the rationalists who are blamed; all philosophers who, racking their brains over the anomalies of the universe, evolve systems which purport to reconcile them, are censurable—censurable, that is to say, if they regard their fictions as having some pretensions to truth. And what philosopher does not? Certainly not Pascal. Selecting from the chaotic mass of concrete experience certain aspects which appeared to him to be interesting, the rest he magnificently ignores. The interesting aspects become Body, Mind and Charity, three vicious abstractions "which have no existence outside the classifying intellect'.

These are erected by Pascal into actual entities in whose reality he actually came to believe. The rest, all

[1] He has for the purposes of his present argument conveniently forgotten that he has already warned us that 'science' also 'is no truer than common sense or lunacy, than art or religion'. See quotation on p. 73. But let this pass. If you are prepared to deny the validity of reason, you cannot be expected to trouble yourself with the bugbear of consistency. See the quotation below, p. 118.

that does not fit in with the three Pascalian absolutes, is explained away.

A Philosophy merely a State of Mind. It is a familiar complaint. The philosopher, whatever his school, constructs a rigid system and uses it as a Procrustean bed into which to fit the infinite variety of nature and experience; if they will not fit, so much the worse for nature and experience. But the system has no reality outside the philosopher's mind; it does not apply to anything, and the historic figures of Truth, Goodness and Beauty, or (as in Pascal) Body, Mind and Charity, with which it is adorned, are lay figures. From the familiar complaint is drawn a familiar moral. Observe phenomena, correlate them, construct formulæ which describe them and enable you to predict others like them; follow, in short, the methods of science, and you may rest assured that your results will be true at least of something. But, as soon as you sit back in your chair and reflect upon the nature of the universe in the light of the results, your conclusions are of interest only to the psychologist. They tell us about you, not about reality. A philosophy is not an account of the universe; it is the symptom of a state of mind. Such, in brief, is Huxley's criticism. It is—it is obvious—fundamental; it is not directed against this philosophy or that, against Pascal because he believed in the objects of his revelation or Descartes in the products of his rationalizing; it is a criticism of the aims and methods of philosophy in general, and of its claim to give an account of the universe in particular. It is this criticism which I propose in this chapter to try to meet.

Like Huxley I too have the habit of pencilling reflections in margins. Huxley's article on Pascal provoked a number. This essay is made up of them. Huxley is only incidentally its subject.

The 'Tu Quoque' Retort. The obvious retort assumes the form of a *tu quoque*. Must not Huxley himself, in denying the validity of systems, assert the very thing he denies? Are not the rationalizing methods he indicts the methods upon which his own indictment is based? Probably they are. Huxley is convinced that philosophical conclusions constructed by processes of reasoning on a remote basis of sense experience do not apply to anything. But how does he reach this conclusion? Apparently by process of reasoning from sense experience. He is using excellent philosophical arguments in defence of a philosophical position. The fact that the position consists in the assertion that all philosophical positions are a reflection of the self and not a transcript of reality, and that the arguments which he uses are devoted to showing that philosophical arguments are vicious rationalizations of instinctive wishes, does not in the least detract from the philosophical character of his achievement. It merely stultifies it. Following a well-known philosophical method—it is as old as the Greeks, and in direct line of descent from the Sophists—Huxley reaches the conclusion that philosophical methods are fallacious; the conclusions to which they lead do not give us truth about reality. Then he should not follow them. Nevertheless he does so continually and not only to discomfit the rationalists, for he has tried, he tells us, to frame a way of life and to draw what he calls a map of reality. But how does he know that it is not merely a map of his own mind?

The point is an obvious one, yet I hesitate to press it. To show that a writer's assertions are inconsistent is not to disprove them, and the scoring of purely logical points is apt to irritate the reader, particularly the English reader, more than the writer against whom they are directed, especially if he is Huxley. For the charge of inconsistency is one which quite peculiarly fails to wring Huxley's withers. On the contrary, he glories in it. 'For me the pleasures of living and understanding have come to outweigh the pleasures . . . of pretending to be consistent. . . . Therefore I indulge my inconsistencies', 'investing myself at the same time with an invulnerable armour against critics'—he might have added, but refrained.

Forbearing to press the logical point, I cannot leave it without asking Huxley to draw for my benefit a distinction between philosophy and science.

Why is Science Immune? Science, it is clear, escapes the gravamen of Huxley's indictment. It does not, he thinks, like philosophy, attempt to prescribe to reality; it is content to record it. Modestly it observes facts, and predicts other facts not yet observed. Certainly it does; but is this all that it does? Certainly not! Science works up its observations into general formulæ, reasons about

them, and draws what purport to be universally applicable conclusions. Biologists, for example (many of
them), tell us that acquired characteristics cannot be
inherited; physiologists (most of them), that an entity
called the soul does not leave the body at death; psychologists (some of them), that mind action will ultimately
be completely interpretable in terms of brain and nerve
action, of which it is a determined function; bio-chem-
ists, that there is no line of demarcation between the
living and the non-living. These conclusions may or
may not be true. But how are they reached? By process
of ratiocination upon the evidence supplied by the
senses. But, if the scientist spends, and rightly, much of
his time in inferring the nature of what has not been
observed on the basis of what has, if he goes further and
generalizes about the characteristics of certain departments of reality not completely explored and the capacities and limitations of certain entities not yet completely
catalogued, by what right does he escape Huxley's
strictures? Is he not like the philosopher prescribing to
reality in the interests of his own predilections and,
when he goes beyond the immediate evidence of his
senses, using his reason to invent arguments for the beliefs which he instinctively wishes to hold? But, Huxley
will say, the scientist's conclusions can be verified, the
philosopher's cannot. But how if the scientist unconsciously cooks the evidence which is required to verify
his conclusions? I shall return to this point later.

Now it *may*, of course, be the case that all our beliefs
are the offspring of our instincts, and that thinking is to

be explained by the fact that we have an instinct, one of the strongest, to find reasons for what we instinctively wish to believe. If this is the case, if we are always constrained by our dispositions and never by the evidence, we are none of us immune, and the scientist sins no less than the philosopher. But is it? I do not think that it is, and here I come to the main point at issue.

The Truth of Rationalism. Huxley's essays contain a criticism of two rather different philosophical positions, that of the rationalists and that of the mystics. Each purports to be a way of obtaining truth about the universe: Rationalism asserts that you can reach truth by process of correct reasoning from premises perceived to be self-evident; Mysticism by process of direct revelation. Huxley does not always distinguish between these two positions, and it is not always clear against which of them his criticisms are being levelled. In fact, however, they are sufficiently distinct, and may be opposed. Pascal, for example, as Mr. Huxley points out, denounced Rationalism and affirmed the validity of mystical revelation. Personally I think the opposition a false one, as I shall try to show, but it will be convenient to take each position separately and to see how far it can be defended against Huxley's somewhat indiscriminate charge of vicious subjectivism.

Rationalism, it is clear, assumes that the universe is at any rate in part reasonable; if it were not, reasoning would not help us to understand it. Now Huxley says bluntly that it is not: 'What', he asks, 'is the final, the

The Truth of Rationalism

theological reason for grass being green and sunflowers yellow?' Admittedly there is none. 'Grass', he says, 'is green because that is how we see it; in other words, it's green because it is green.' Huxley proceeds to infer that what is true of the greenness of grass is true of all the other characteristics of the universe. Things are green because they are; similarly they are agonizing or pleasant, holy or shameful, beautiful or ugly, because they are, and that is all there is to it. The universe for Huxley is all of a piece, and if you want to know what it is like, you must go and look. Inevitably, since, if the universe is irrational, there is no other way. All our knowledge, in other words, comes to us through sense experience, and is limited by sense experience.

Now this is simply not true. Some of our knowledge does not come to us through sense experience. It may, of course, be illustrated by sense experience, and *some* sense experience may be necessary before we realize that we have it, but it is other than the knowledge given to us by our senses and outruns it. It is this knowledge that we call *a priori*, and by it rationalists have set store —naturally, since it is only reason that can give it to us, and *of* what is reasonable that we can have it. Mathematical and logical knowledge are pre-eminently of this character. That two sides of a triangle are greater than the third, that two plus two make four, that the whole is greater than the part, that if P implies Q, and Q implies R, then P implies R, that A must either be A or not A, these are general propositions which are true; and that they are true is known otherwise than through the senses

III. Aldous Huxley and the Dowagers

Sense experience, no doubt, is necessary to draw our attention to them. The child plays with bricks and beans, takes two pairs, puts them together and counts four. The particular truth must be realized on a number of occasions before the general one is grasped. But once this has been done, it is realized that the truth that two and two make four is true not only of the particular objects counted, but of all objects in the universe, both those which have been counted and those which have not; not only of those things which exist in the present, but of any things that may come to exist in the future; in short, of any things whatever. What is more, even if no objects existed, even if, that is to say, there were no particular things for us to experience and for it to apply to, the general proposition that two plus two make four would, it is realized, still be true and could still be known by mind. Thus, though sense experience may be necessary to draw our attention to the truth, the truth itself is seen to be independent of such experience. It is not, therefore, by means of sense experience that it is known. How then? Presumably by our reasons. The truth once grasped is seen to be necessary and inevitable. Our reasons could not conceive it otherwise; therefore it is so.

That knowledge of such truths exists is obvious. The point is an elementary one and should not require stressing, were it not that Huxley seems to have overlooked it. Overlooked by Huxley, it was embraced with acclamation by the rationalists. Impressed by the fact that there were some truths about the universe which were directly apprehended by reason, and for the trustworthiness of which the testimony of reason was a sufficient guarantee, they proceeded to assume that all our knowledge was of the same character, that all the characteristics of the universe could be discovered by the same method.

Excesses of Rationalism. Now if the universe were like a mathematical problem, the assumption would be justified. Just as a mathematician sitting at his desk could, provided he reasoned well enough, deduce the whole of mathematics from a few self-evident propositions, so the philosopher at ease in his chair could, provided he philosophized well enough, arrive at the complete truth about the universe by meditating upon the nature of his own experience. Inferring the nature of what is from the nature of what must (according to reason) be, he would be absolved from the necessity of checking his results by observation. It would be unnecessary, in other words, for him to go and see whether the universe which he had inferred was in the least like the universe that is. Many philosophers have in fact proceeded on these lines and with the distressing results which Huxley justly derides. Meditating in their arm-chairs they have produced maps of the universe on which nobody else has been able to find his way. Inevitably, since the maps were maps not of the universe but of the philosophers. Like Huxley, these rationalist philosophers have assumed that the universe is all of a piece. Unfortunately the universe is not like a mathematical problem, and the method of Rationalism, admissible in the realm of logic and mathematics, fails completely to tell us what exists in the world of fact. 'What I clearly and distinctly conceive is true', said Descartes. Very likely, but it does not therefore *exist*. There is no reason whatever why a substance with the specific gravity of gold should be yellow. Hence we cannot discover the fact by reasoning; we must go and look—in other words, we must follow the method commended by Huxley. We arrive, then, at the conclusion that, so far as the world revealed to sense experience is concerned, neither Rationalism nor any other philosophy can tell us what it contains. If we want to know, we must experience it.

Universe not all of a Piece. But it does not therefore follow that Rationalism is valueless, and it does not follow precisely because the universe is not all of a piece. Herein lies Huxley's mistake. Seeing that there is nothing reasonable about the fact that grass is green, he infers there is nothing reasonable about the fact that the whole is greater than the part. He is wrong. The truth of the matter is that certain regions of the universe are separated by real differences in kind. There are, in short, to put it crudely, two worlds—two at least, possibly more. There is, first, the world of sense experience; this is the home of irrationality and contingency, and its contents can only be discovered, if at all, by inspection; and there is, secondly, the world of necessity, the home of reason, the nature of which is revealed in thinking to mind. The experience of our senses will no more provide us with information about this second world than reason can inform us of the characteristics of the first.

What are the contents of this second world? Here we enter the realm of controversy. Many, as I have said, have considered it to be all-inclusive, and proceeded to impugn the reality of the arbitrary, haphazard facts which refused to fit into it. Rejecting the view that the universe is reasonable throughout, we may nevertheless still ask whether the second world, the world of necessity, is limited by the realms of logic and mathematics. What of ethics and æsthetics? At this point I must make a confession. Many, perhaps most philosophers—and I hope that it will not set the reader against them—have claimed that Goodness and Beauty must, with Truth, be included in the second world. Huxley, as we have seen, denies this claim. Beauty, Goodness and Truth are for him fictions invented to gratify human desires. How are we to make it good?

Here arises a difficulty. That there is a distinction between the two worlds I affirm, and reason, I affirm further, can give us true information about the second. But how are we to draw the line between them? Reason alone, it is clear, can draw it. Hence reason is in the position of being both judge and jury in her own cause.

Assuming complete domination over the second world, claiming it as her own, she arrogates to herself the right to prescribe its boundaries. The position seems unsatisfactory, for reason, when pressed to show cause why this or that should be included in her world, seems unable to produce her title deeds. There is, in other words,

III. Aldous Huxley and the Dowagers

no proof that certain propositions which are known *a priori* are true and that they assert facts which are real, and only proof, it seems, will give Huxley satisfaction.

The Limits of Proof. But there are many things which Huxley accepts without proof, the validity of inference for example. All reasoning, it is obvious, depends upon the principle of induction. If I am not entitled to assume that the more frequently A and B have been found together in the past, the greater the probability that A will be accompanied by B in the future, if I am not entitled, applying this principle, to infer A from B, or to say that A follows from B, or to affirm that A is implied by B, I cannot reason at all, for a chain of reasoning is nothing but a set of inferences. Not only can I not reason, I cannot live. The gong rings for dinner, and I descend to the dining-room. Why? Because the dining-room and food having been frequently found in association in the past, I infer that they will be so associated in the future. If I did not unconsciously make this inference, I might just as well ascend to the roof or stay where I am. In either event I should not eat, and if I do not eat I die.

The legitimacy of induction is assumed, it is clear, not only in reasoning, but in every moment of our daily life. We think on the assumption that it is valid and we act on the assumption that it is valid. But how is its validity to be established? Certainly not by reasoning, for that would be to assume the validity of the very principle that it is required to prove; nor by sense experience, for induction is equally entailed by sense experience, enabling us, for example, to work up the chaos of sense data of which our senses make us aware into a coherent world of chairs and tables. It seems, then, that we have got to assume it. Reason again is both judge and jury in her own cause. Asserting that she is unable to function unless she is allowed to infer, she gives herself permission to infer.

The truth of the principle of induction—it is a nettle we must grasp sooner or later, and we may as well grasp it now—is, in fact, revealed to insight. We just see that A follows from B, and that is all we can say. Does Huxley, therefore, doubt the principle? Not at all. It is rampant throughout the whole of his closely reasoned essay. But if the principle of induction, upon which the whole structure of reasoning rests, is revealed to insight, may not other things be so revealed? What other things?

Those to which I have already referred as the dowagers of philosophy, Truth, Goodness and Beauty. Huxley, as I have had already to confess, is extremely rude to the dowagers, so rude, in fact, as to refuse to recognize their existence. Metaphysically he cuts them dead. It is high time that somebody spoke up for their reputation, and though I am in general not much given to the defence of dowagers, my chivalry urges me to take up Huxley's challenge.

Insight and Reason. Let me begin by summarizing the conclusions I have reached. First, there are some truths which cannot be proved; they are nevertheless true.

III. Aldous Huxley and the Dowagers

For these truths it is inadmissible to demand evidence, for they are self-evident. They are, that is to say, simply seen to be true and unquestioningly accepted as such. Among them is the truth of the principle of inference or induction, which Huxley accepts.

Secondly, to the degree that all reasoning rests upon the principle of induction, reasoning has an irrational basis. Not only is the general principle accepted without proof, but each step of the argument which the principle leads us to take is strictly indefensible. At each step in a chain of argument we either see that A follows from B, or we do not. If we do not, no arguments can be brought forward to convince us which do not themselves involve similar acts of insight, which do not themselves, that is to say, involve an acceptance of some step similar to that questioned.

The words 'acts of insight' are used deliberately because they lead to my third conclusion, that there is an element of direct revelation in all thinking. We either see things, or we do not. It follows that, since we undoubtedly reason and sometimes reason correctly, there can be no objection in principle to the acceptance of truths instinctively apprehended or revealed to insight. The principle of direct revelation, in other words, may be accepted as a method of arriving at truth.

We are now in a position to take up the cudgels on behalf of the dowagers.

Enough has, I hope, been said to show that no strictly rational defence is possible. Like other dowagers, Truth, Goodness and Beauty are not reasonable. But having agreed that there is nothing against them on principle, let us see what considerations can be advanced in their favour. They are mainly negative. If we cannot positively vindicate the actuality of the dowagers, it is at least possible to show that most of the attacks that are made upon them are baseless. If we cannot prove that Goodness, Truth and Beauty exist, we certainly cannot prove, as Huxley seems to think, that they do not. Let me begin by stating, as I understand it, the precise point at issue.

The Argument from Subjective Need Examined. Certain phenomena of which we are conscious in ethical and æsthetic experience have seemed to many to be explicable only upon the assumption that there are in the universe certain absolute values, Goodness and Beauty, with which the phenomena in question are intimately connected, and from which they derive their significance. Those who have taken this view have tried to show that the assumption of the reality of these values provides the only coherent and intelligible account of the phenomena, and that to that extent their existence is demanded by reason. In the last resort, however, they have admitted that these objective values are revealed only to direct insight or intuition, which in their most satisfying and authoritative forms are vouchsafed to us in mystical vision. Against them it is urged by Huxley that these absolutes are subjective figments projected by our minds into the external world. They are not, therefore, in any sense independently real. The dowagers, in short, are merely Mrs. Harrises.

III. Aldous Huxley and the Dowagers

In the first place, we may ask, what is the precise significance of the word 'subjective' as it is used in this connection? It is, I think, this: if the existence of an entity can be shown to answer to a need of the human spirit, it may be inferred that the entity in question is an assumption of the spirit that needs it. We need, as Mr. Huxley says, a spiritual world more truly real than that of everyday life. Therefore we falsely assume that it exists.

But things are not quite so simple as that. Although the need is subjective, the situation in which it arises is not. Man's consciousness is no isolated and arbitrary phenomenon in the universe, but, as Huxley would be the first to admit, a biological growth moulded by its past and bearing the impress of its origin plainly upon it. What is true of man's consciousness is true also of the needs of his consciousness. These, too, have their roots in the past, are determined by man's ancestry, and conditioned by his environment. Presumably, therefore, they reflect the factors that condition them. Now man's ancestry and his environment, together with all the influences which have gone to make him what he is, are not subjective, but objective. They constitute the external situation in which his consciousness and the needs of his consciousness arise, and to which they respond. This external situation is a real factor in the universe. Hence man's needs, instead of being subjective phenomena, in the sense in which what is subjective is arbitrarily so, spring from and reflect real factors in the universe. There is, therefore, reason to suppose that, when these needs are so widespread as to be almost universal, the universe to which they point should bear a definite relation to the situation in which they have arisen. It would indeed be strange, if a need which was demonstrably the product of a real situation, should be devoid both of point and significance, and own no objective counterpart in the universe which gave it birth.

The Argument from 'Origins' Examined. Secondly, it is important to realize precisely how much and also how little the argument from the origins of human needs proves. On this point there is much current misconception. Tracing the beginning of the æsthetic consciousness in the emotions and of the moral consciousness in the social observances of primitive tribes, people argue as if in so doing they had somehow discredited or invalidated the æsthetic and moral consciousness. It is not clear why. If the doctrine of evolution is to be taken seriously, we are surely entitled to hold that there is more in the evolved product than there was in the germ from which it may be shown to have arisen. Why should this doctrine not apply to the phenomena of the developed human consciousness? To show that religion began as Totemism and Exogamy does not prove that it is not religion, that is to say, something very different now, any more than the discovery that the savage can only count on the fingers of one hand invalidates the multiplication table. To know that Einstein was once a fish and still possesses the rudiments of gills tells us very little about the present mind of Einstein. To judge a thing by its fruits is as relevant to an estimation of its true character as to judge it by its roots. It is as important, in other words, to know what a thing is aiming at as to know how it began, and no account of it which, looking to its origin, proceeds to interpret its present nature solely in terms of its early history, can pretend to be complete. In any event it cannot be too strongly emphasized that to lay bare the origin of a thing is not tantamount to discrediting it. The point should be obvious, yet Huxley often argues as if the fact that savages have believed in God constitutes a sufficient ground for regarding God as a figment, just as in writing of Pascal he seems to think that by showing that Goodness, Truth and Beauty reflect present needs, and that these present needs have developed by a continuous process from savage ones, he has somehow proved Goodness, Truth and Beauty to be unreal. Because everybody believes and has always believed in something, the belief admittedly is not therefore true; but equally it is not therefore false.

What, then, is Real? Thirdly, we are entitled to ask by what criterion of reality that of the dowagers is impugned. If they are not real, what is? As far as I can gather, Huxley's answer—as it is certainly the answer of many similar critics—is that the physical world of which our senses make us aware is real. Huxley often writes as if the world of material objects and the mind which knows it are the only types of reality that exist.

What, then, is Real?

Nothing that is not matter or mind—and even mind may turn out to be merely a function of matter—is for him real. I am surprised that Huxley should subscribe to this common-sense notion of reality. He argues at times as if he were unaware that common sense is merely a mass of dead metaphysics; its beliefs the debris left by the philosophies of the past. Yet he should know—no one better—that there are very good reasons indeed for denying that the everyday matter-of-fact world has any existence independent of ourselves. And he does know it, for he tells us in his Essays that mind may be the creator of matter, and flirts engagingly with the solipsist hypothesis that we never know anything except our own mental states. Admitting so much, how can he bring himself to employ the so-called 'reality' of the sensible world known to us in perception as a stick with which to chastise the dowagers? Unless we are prepared to take an extremely naïve view of perception, for which modern science holds no brief, it is not in the external world of daily experience that we are to find the objective reality which is denied to revealed values.

For it is not merely agnosticism that modern science professes as to the nature of the objects of our perception. If it were, the case from Huxley's point of view would be bad, but not so bad. But science does not assert that it cannot tell us what is the nature of the reality of what we perceive. On the contrary, physicists are surprisingly found to detect in the apparently neutral objects of everyday experience, precisely what Huxley detects in the world of spiritual values, namely ourselves. The modern scientist, in fact, has made a belated discovery of the uses of Idealism, and is surprised to have to announce what many philosophers could have told him all along, that his so-called external world is a projection of himself. We only know our own ideas and sensations, said Locke, Berkeley and Hume; the external cause of these ideas and sensations is unknown to us, said Berkeley, Hume and (with reservations) Locke, and must be presumed to be God (Berkeley) or non-existent (Hume). We know only the phenomenal world, the part product of our mental categories, said Kant. Things as they are in themselves, if there be such, we do not know.

The Scientists discover Idealism. Emanating merely from philosophers, these assertions attracted little attention. It is only since the voices of the physicist and psychologist have been raised to swell the idealist chorus that the part which we ourselves play in constructing our own perceptual world has been generally conceded. To many psychologists the advance of psychology seems to yield continuous evidence that the more closely we analyse the objects of our consciousness, the more certainly do we find ourselves. 'We make our own world,' says Havelock Ellis; 'when we have made it awry we can remake it approximately truer. Man lives by imagination.' And Vaïhinger has urged that just as the digestive system breaks up the matter which it receives, mixes it with its own juices and so makes it suitable for assimilation in the practical interests of the organism, 'so the psyche envelops the thing perceived with categories which it has developed out of itself.' Thus our consciousness is no guide whatever to the physical happenings, if any, outside our skins.

The physicist is in substantial agreement. The theory of relativity, for instance, has much to say of the mental factor in scientific explanation. The physicist's world is a spatio-temporal flux of events whose characteristics are limited to severely mathematical properties. Upon them the mind imposes, or from them it selects (accounts differ) certain patterns which appear to possess the quality of comparative permanence. These patterns are worked up by the mind into continuing objects, and become the chairs and tables of daily life. But, as they are modelled by the mind, so do they reflect the needs of the perceiver. Different minds with different interests, those of Martians for example, selecting different patterns would 'perceive' different worlds. 'All through the physical world', says Eddington, 'runs an unknown content, which must really be the stuff of our own consciousness. . . . We have found that where science has progressed the farthest, the mind has but regained from nature that which the mind has put into nature.'

Chairs and the Dowagers on all Fours. Is not the language familiar? Do we not recognize the authentic subjectivist note? *Mutatis mutandis*, the words might be those of Huxley disclosing, as if it were some shameful secret, the human origin of the dowagers. Human in origin they may be, but, if they are, chairs and tables are in the same case, and for the same reason.

Does Huxley deny the reality of chairs and tables? Apparently not! Matter, he says, 'whether we like it or not, is always there'. With what logic then does he deny the reality of absolute values formed apparently by the same process of mental projection? The difference between a chair and a philosophical dowager is merely the difference between the ways in which our experience is organized. We organize our sensory experience and produce the world of material objects which science explores; we organize our spiritual experience and, behold, the dowagers Goodness, Truth and Beauty, whom philosophers discuss and whom mystics enjoy. Whatever grounds there are for impugning the independent reality of the second world are equally valid against that of the first. But if, rejecting these grounds, we hold that what we perceive by the senses is objectively real and exists independently of our experience, then what we perceive by the spirit is equally so. Personally I do reject them, but that is another matter which cannot be pursued here. I mention it only to explain my support of the dowagers.

Application to Mystical Experience. But Huxley has a further point. If we were to assume provisionally that absolute values are real, that they are independent of ourselves and not projections of ourselves, then, he says, we could not know them. Why not? 'The revelations', he says, speaking of mystical experience, 'are couched in human language and are the work of individual human beings who lived all too humanly in space and time. We are fatally back again among the relativities.' This seems to be a simple confusion between a revelation and its object. Granted for the moment that the object of mystical experience, though revealed to insight, is independent of it, that it is discovered not created, then the fact that it is described in human language is no ground for inferring that it itself is human. The mystic, no doubt, talks nonsense; at least it is nonsense to those who are not mystics. But how could it be otherwise? Language was invented to describe the objects of one world, the world of common experience, and to communicate its happenings. It is clearly inappropriate to those of another. If there is a world of absolute values, any attempt to discourse of it in the language of the common-sense world must of necessity be misleading; at any rate it will mislead all who have not shared in some degree the experience to which it relates. I cannot, if I may revert to the toothache, convey by means of words the experience of a toothache to one who has never had it; but that does not mean that my toothache is not real. Similarly the fact that the mystics' accounts of the dowagers are vague and flowery to the nth degree, gives no reason for supposing that the dowagers have not been viewed. If mysticism could give an account of itself, it would cease to be mysticism.

Mr. Huxley's language at this point is itself confused, but I am inclined to think that it conveys a suggestion to the effect that, if the inhuman and perfect existed, the human and relative could have no intercourse with it. I agree that it could not, if intercourse implied continuity of substance and community of being. The perfect, it is clear, could not enter into communion with the imperfect. But why should the relationship imply communion in this sense? One does not after all have intercourse with dowagers. But one can contemplate them. A cat may look at a king, and a mystic at a dowager, and neither the king nor the dowager is any the worse for the experience. They are probably unaware of it.

Chapter V

Defence of Reason—I. Reason and Truth

★

I. ATTACK ON REASON

Reason the Tool of Impulse and Desire. I propose to begin in this chapter the defence of reason to which I committed myself in the third. The contemporary disparagement takes two main forms. There are those who assert that in the realm of thought reason does not and cannot give us the truth, and those who in the realm of conduct declare that reason should not, even if it can, guide our lives. Both forms of attack have in recent years derived considerable impetus from the growth of psycho-analysis and the popularization of the notions which psycho-analysts have made familiar. The animal origin of human nature is emphasized and the fact that our roots stretch back to a remote pre-human past. It is from these roots, it is said, that the continuous stream of impulses and desires which is the driving force of our actions takes its rise. Impulses and desires are the springs not only of conduct but also of thought. The energy with which we think, no less than the energy with which we act is, therefore, non-rational in origin. And not only the energy, but also the incentive. For thinking no less than

acting is undertaken with a purpose; it is prompted by
the desire to reach a conclusion. The desire for a conclusion determines the character and trend of our
thinking. Hence, the goal which attracts, no less than
the energy which inspires our apparently rational
activities is irrational. If impulse is the motive force
which drives reason from behind, it is difficult not to
suppose that reason will march to the tune that impulse
pipes her. If goals and ends are the prizes that pull
reason from in front, it is difficult not to believe that she
will reach only those conclusions which are compatible
with their achievement. Thus reason comes increasingly
to be represented not as a free activity, moving disinterestedly in accordance with the laws which she herself has dictated to the dispassionate contemplation of
ends which only she can conceive, but as a servant of
irrational forces suborned by them to reach the goal,
whether of action or belief, that will afford them the
greatest instinctive satisfaction.

In pursuance of this role, reason invents arguments
for what we instinctively wish to believe and pretexts
for what we instinctively wish to do. Morality itself
may be, and frequently is, interpreted in this way.
Laws and codes, conventions and prohibitions are screens
erected by society to disguise from its members the real
nature of their motives. Englishmen, it is said, have
brought the use of reason to an unusual degree of efficiency in the performance of this office, and are never at
a loss for an argument to convince themselves that they
are only doing their duty, whenever they want an

excuse for making themselves disagreeable. Thus Samuel Butler tells us of his father that he never would admit that he did anything because he wanted to; he was always able to persuade himself that what he wanted to do was also what he ought to do.

Impotence of Reason in Action and Thought. The fisherman who persuades himself that fish being cold-blooded animals do not really feel the pain of having their throats dragged out of them by a hook, the parent who believes that he flogs his child for its good and not for his pleasure, the smoker who assures us that tobacco ash is good for the carpet, no less than the nation which pretends that it is fighting to maintain the integrity of treaties, to make the world safe for democracy, to preserve its honour, its place in the sun, its wives, children, firesides, religion or what not, whenever it wants an excuse to indulge its impulses of aggression and destruction, are all, it is said, in their own ways utilizing their reasons to justify them in indulging their passions. It is, indeed, the chief difference between the civilized man and the savage, that the former is under the necessity of invoking his reason to assure himself that he is doing his individual or civic duty by judicially murdering criminals, patriotically hating foreigners, or 'lynching' negroes in a passion of moral indignation, whenever he wants an excuse for gratifying instincts which savages indulge without hypocrisy.

As in action, so in thought. 'Metaphysics', said Bradley, may be 'the finding of bad reasons for what we believe upon instinct'; but 'to find these reasons is no less an instinct'. Science is represented as the product of the impulse of curiosity, philosophy of that of wonder, art of that of play. As for religion, it is simply a contrivance on the part of reason for satisfying our unconscious need to think that the universe is at heart friendly to human nature, and that the spiritual, the minded and the akin condition and underly the brutal, the mindless and the alien. Thus reason, together with conscience and will, together in fact with all the more conscious and lately acquired faculties of the race, is regarded as a screen for our instincts, an apologist for our passions and a tool of our needs. It is a cork bobbing about on the waves of unconscious impulses whose direction is determined by the currents that run below the surface.

Reason as the Cancer of the Soul. Impotent in the sphere of thought, reason is represented as deleterious in that of practice. The life of the philosopher or the scholar which men in the past have consented to admire even when they could not hope to emulate, is to-day decried because it does not give scope to our passions and impulses. Under the influence of D. H. Lawrence and similar writers, men have come to think that thinking is almost a crime. Not only must we not pass our lives reading in the library or observing in the laboratory; we must not even permit reason to guide them in the home or the market place. To do so is to do violence to our 'real' nature by damming up the stream of impulses and desires in which it resides. Upon this 'real' nature reason is treated as a sort of excrescence, which has grown and spread until it has sucked into itself all the energies of our being. It is represented as absorbing for its own nourishment the generous forces of man's passional nature, thus depriving the organism as a whole of the primitive energy which alone can give zest and love of living. Reason has in fact become a cancer preying upon the tissues of the soul. Hence, the life according to reason comes to be regarded as a kind of bloodless abstraction from life proper, and we are asked in the interests of full, free and fruitful living to restrain not the passions but the reason.

The Cult of the Primitive. In contemporary literature this attack upon the reason takes two rather different forms. At Huxley's intellectual anti-rationalism we have already glanced. There remains the romantic anti-rationalism of Lawrence.

One of the outstanding developments of the post-war years has been a revolt against sophistication and a romantic cult of the primitive. The post-war repudiation of the traditional disciplines in conduct has been accompanied by a repudiation of traditional disciplines in art. Negroes and jazz, the emanation of negroes; the jungle and the Ju-Ju and Epstein's statues, the emanation of the jungle and the Ju-Ju; the music of Stravinsky and the pictures of the Surréalistes are acclaimed just because they are *not* in the classical tradition, because they do *not* embody the traditional æsthetic virtues, the virtues of clarity and poise and studied beauty of form.

I. Reason and Truth

M. Breton writing in *The Quarter*, an American review which has devoted a whole number to the exposition of Surréalism, expresses his belief 'in the higher reality of certain forms of association hitherto neglected, in the omnipotence of dreaming, in the unbiassed play of thought'. To this unexplored territory he welcomes artists and creative writers, suggesting that it is the matrix of all true art. 'Artists and creative writers' are not slow to accept the invitation. Nerval gives us poems whose exploration of the vague territories of the subliminal issues via a fabric of unconscious association in phrases and rhythms that derive their meaning, if any, from the forgotten past, and apparently make their appearance on the poet's writing paper as unaccountably as spirit messages, which, indeed, they often resemble, while Salvador Duli offers us pictures in which, against a predominating background of grand pianos, the skulls of animals, entrails, fœtuses and alarmingly distorted human beings jostle one another in their efforts to portray the enigmatic pulsings of the subliminal self.

The Divine Abdomen of Lawrence. Of this cult D. H. Lawrence is at once the apologist and the priest. He has given it its most notable literary expression; he has also provided it with its Bible. Going to Mexico to get local colour for his revolt against civilization, he found the perfect type of humanity in men in whom the intellect was demonstrably subordinate to the stomach, the genitals and the solar plexus. The perfect Lawrencian man has subjected his intellect to these fundamental organs and to the psychological growths which are rooted in them; indeed, it is not too much to say that his intellect is literally in his guts. This, at least, seems to be the meaning of those lyrical passages in which Lawrence raves over a dusky 'abdomen where the great blood stream surges in the dark and surges in its own generic experience . . . it is the dark blood falling back from the mind, from sight and speech and knowing, back to the great central source where is rest and unspeakable renewal'. Abjuring as artificial reason and the life of the intellect, subsiding into 'the great blood stream which surges in the dark' of the abdomen and the genitals, man renews his being and becomes one with the ultimate reality of things.

And the ultimate reality of things? It is nothing more nor less than God. Hence, to abjure the intellect is to become divine. 'I can become one with God, consummated into eternity,' Lawrence declares, 'by taking the road down the senses into the utter darkness of power, till I am one with the darkness of initial power, beyond knowledge of any opposite.' The last phrase has a familiar ring. We seem to be listening to the cry of one of the great Christian mystics, to Madame Guyon or St. John of the Cross, struggling through the 'Dark Night of the Soul'. 'Everywhere one Being, one Life' was the goal of mystical activity towards which the self struggled in the dimness and anguish of the 'Dark Night': 'Thereupon speaks the Heavenly Father to him, "Thou shalt call me Father, and shalt never cease to enter in, ever nearer, so as to sink the deeper in an unhuman and un-named abyss; and, above all ways, images and forms, and above all powers, to lose thyself, deny thyself, and ever unform thyself." In this last condition nothing is to be seen but a ground which rests upon itself, everywhere one Being, one Life.' So Tauler, describing the drastic process of unselfing, the abdication of reason and con-sciousness which in the 'Dark Night of the Soul' paves the way for union with the Divine. . . .

But what for the mystics was a painful and humiliat-ing prerequisite of union, a stage one had regrettably to undergo, is apparently for Lawrence the goal itself. While they looked upwards for the divine, finding the uniting thread in the ecstasies of the developed spirit, Lawrence looks downwards and finds it in the orgasms of the excited genitals. The consciousness of the enrap-tured mystic is lost in God; that of Lawrence's idealized Mexican with 'face lifted and sightless, eyes half closed and visionless, mouth open and speechless' is sunk in 'the abdomen'. The intellect, if not the spirit, may, Lawrence concedes, win free from these subterranean influences; but it does so at its peril. In fact all the features of modern civilization which he most dislikes are due to the disastrous fact that it has in a measure won free. For the price of its freedom is to cut itself off from the 'central source' of being. Hence the life of the mind is like the life of an uprooted flower, arid, sterile and short.

Sentimentality Inverted. Now this belly worship seems to

me to spring from a source entirely different from that of the sophisticated Huxleyan relativism at which I have already glanced. Mark Rampion, in *Point Counterpoint*, is, indeed sometimes acclaimed as an embodiment of Lawrence, or at least a mouthpiece for the characteristically Lawrencian point of view. And Rampion, it is said, is presented sympathetically; he is one of the least repulsive people in the book. Possibly! Nevertheless, Lawrence's doctrine owns different roots from Huxley's, is inspired by different motives and issues in a different creed. Huxley's is an impartial, an all-round sort of philosophy. He is for giving all sides of our nature a fair show. He does not discriminate against reason; he merely denies its primacy and warns us against allowing it to be sole guide to our conduct or supposing that it can give us truth. Lawrence would like to submerge it altogether.

And yet the influences upon contemporary life and thought of these two such different gospels of two such different men are not dissimiliar. Each seeks to dethrone reason from the seat which has been traditionally claimed for her by that great line of European thinkers which stretches from Plato to Mill. Each is readily acclaimed by an unromantic generation which, headed off by the excesses of the Victorians and the mockings of Shaw from the traditional outlets for its sentimentality in brooks and roses, baa-lambs and larks, hymns and angels, must invert its values and find a mystical significance in fœtuses and intestines and a new channel for its romanticism in the blood stream, the solar plexus and the unconscious. Each has contributed his quota to the anti-rationalism of the age.

Claude Houghton on Emotional Death. This anti-rationalism pervades our literature. Scarcely a novel is written with any claim to serious attention that does not implicitly or explicitly endorse it. Hemingway writes deliberately in words of one syllable arranged in sentences of not more than a dozen words, for fear that he might tax the intelligences of his readers, or impute to them a shameful sophistication by presuming their familiarity with the rotundities of classical English prose. William Faulkner chooses characters whose minds and emotions are alike of an extreme simplicity. In a series of books, *The Crisis, I am Jonathan Scrivener, Chaos is Come Again,* and most notably in *Julian Grant Loses his Way,* Claude Houghton, widely acclaimed as one of the most 'representative' and one of the most 'significant'—blessed meaning-begging words!—novelists of the day, joins in the anti-rational hue and cry. I suppose that the word 'representative' means that Houghton stands for and expresses the tendencies now stirring in the minds of typical young men of to-day; 'significant' may mean expressive of those not yet stirring, but about to stir. Houghton is, therefore, not only a reflection but a signpost.

And what does he reflect? To what does he point? To the terrible fate that awaits the follower of logic. *Julian Grant* is the epitome of a man's life, the life of a man who, setting logic, curiosity, the lust of knowledge and the greed of experience (I am not sure, on reflection, that Huxley, let alone Lawrence, would like the anim-adversion implied in 'the greed of experience') above love and pity and intuitive understanding, loses his way, wanders in spiritual bogs, and finally 'dies an emotional death'.

Dying 'an emotional death' does not mean, as one might have been tempted to suppose, dying in an emotional manner. What it does mean apparently is suffering a death of the emotions. Those emotionally dead no longer feel anything at all!

I am not clear precisely why an emotional death so defined should be regarded with such horror—one would have thought that, in so far as one's feelings were unpleasant (and too many feelings are) it would be rather nice to contrive not to have them; although how the most 'emotionally dead' man would be able not to feel a dentist's drill, or the fear of it, or being flogged to death in a German concentration camp, or the fear of it, we are not told—but there is no doubt that to Houghton and his school it is the most terrible thing that can hap-pen to a man. It is equivalent to loss of honour by a Victorian middle-class woman; that is, it is worse, much worse, than death *tout court*.

Indictment of Reason Summarized. But in spite of the vagueness of Houghton's message, its general purport is clear enough. Julian Grant is an epitome of his civiliz-ation, a civilization that has trusted overmuch to intel-lect and now drifts to chaos because of the disparity between its intellect and its spirit. Pride of intellect is censured; spiritual humility approved. The heart has its reasons of which the reason knows nothing; and they are good reasons. Logic is a bad guide, feeling is a good one. Let us, therefore, at all costs stop thinking and try to feel. As Chesterton has told us, 'It is better to talk wisdom foolishly like a saint, than to babble folly wisely like a don.'

Again, I am not sure how far Huxley would approve this particular form of the current anti-rationalism. That slighting reference to 'greed of experience' for example, seems to traverse one of his favourite doctrines. One can almost see him wince, as that favourite corn, 'Give them all a show', is trodden on. But with the general trend of the indictment of reason, he would, as we have seen in previous chapters, find little to quarrel. And since he is at once the most lucid and the most influential of the anti-rationalists, it will be as well to return for a summary and succinct statement of the modern anti-rationalist case to his writings.

The indictment might, then, read somewhat as follows. First, reason never gives us theoretical truth— 'Science', it will be remembered, is 'no truer than common sense or lunacy, than art or religion', since 'even if one should correspond to things in themselves as perceived by some hypothetical non-human being, it would be impossible for us to discover which it was'. Secondly, to allow reason to rule the soul is to commit an offence against life:—'To live, the soul must be in intimate contact with the world; must assimilate it through all the channels of sense and desire, thought and feeling, which nature has provided for the purpose.'

The Pitiable Intellectual. Now this precisely is what, according to Huxley, the intellectual does not do. The scholar, the philosopher, the recluse, even the scientist, are men who have chosen to go through the world halt and maimed. In choosing reason as their guide, knowledge as their goal, they have definitely abjured some of 'the channels of sense and desire', and have scorned delights in order the better to live laborious days. And they are condemned for their pains as pitiable human abstractions. Huxley quotes with appropriate comments the famous passage from the *Phaedo* in which Socrates describes the characteristic austerities of the philosopher. ' "Do you think it like a philosopher to take very seriously what are called pleasures such as eating and drinking?" "Certainly not, Socrates," said Simmias. (How one's feet itch to kick the bottoms of these imbeciles who always agree with the old sophist, whatever nonsense he talks! They deserved the hemlock even more richly than their master.) "Or sex?" Socrates goes on. "No." "Or the whole business of looking after the body? Will the philosopher rate that highly?" Of course he won't—the fool! The philosopher's soul "withdraws itself as far as it can from all association and contact with the body and reaches out after truth by itself". With what results? Deprived of its nourishment, the soul grows thin and mangy, like the starved lion.'

I. Reason and Truth

Nor do the other philosophers fare better. Kant, Newton and Descartes are treated with pitying contempt because, in greater or less measure, they chose to withdraw themselves from the ordinary avocations of life in order to pursue truth. They are stigmatized as 'extraordinary and lamentable souls'. ' "Poor brutes," we cry at the sight of them'. ' "Why aren't they given enough to eat?" ' A little hard this on men who devoted their lives to trying to penetrate the secrets of the universe! Hard, and in the case of Descartes unjust; Descartes, who voluntarily enlisted as a soldier in order to see the world; saw it and saw, too, fighting in the Low Countries; incurred the displeasure of the Church, was threatened with the fate of Galileo, and ultimately died of inflammation of the lungs caught through getting up at five in the morning to teach the Queen of Sweden philosophy. I wonder how often Huxley gets up at five in the morning!

Attitude of my Students. Waiving the somewhat unfortunate illustration of Descartes, we may state Huxley's case as follows. All sides of our nature must be given free and equal play, because all sides of our nature have equal value. To guide one's life by reason and to cultivate one's intelligence, either for its own sake or in order that one may the better guide one's life, is to forgo the development of certain important sides of one's nature. It is in fact to starve oneself, and such starvation is an offence against life. Reasoning and reflecting, we lose contact with the earth and, as Lawrence would add, with our own entrails. Cut off from the natural source of its being, the soul becomes parched and thin, like a plant whose taproot has been severed. The intellectual, in short, lives and thinks in a water-tight compartment which his reason has made for him. So isolated, he is precluded both from living happily and from thinking fruitfully.

This criticism of reason has become part of the intellectual climate of our time. It is implicit in the thought of the age. And, inevitably, the great Victorians are its particular targets. How emphatically my students in their essays denounce such men as Spencer and Mill. How pitiably they depict their lives! They did not get drunk; they were not notorious for the quantity or the exuberance of their affairs with women; they did not set or cultivate new æsthetic fashions; they had no taste in wines; it is most improbable they even overate. Also they did not rush about in cars, go to cocktail parties, play games, thrill at the movies, or consort with young women in beach pyjamas. They only wrote books. What starved, what miserable lives!

Support from Dr. I. A. Richards. The two criticisms of reason that I have outlined, the criticism that it cannot give us truth, and the criticism that its excessive use is inimical to the good life, are at bottom the same criticism. Because truth is conceived to be unobtainable and absolute beauty a chimæra, because in a word no values are recognized external to the self, attention comes to be concentrated upon the self. If the self is the sole object of interest, its welfare becomes the sole object of pursuit. In what does its welfare consist? In goodness of living. What, then, is goodness of living? Can we admit that 'goodness' is a value, when we have so ignominiously jettisoned values from the scheme of things? Certainly we cannot. Goodness of living is simply fullness of living. The best life, then, is the one that satisfies the greatest number of our impulses and desires. Value, in so far as we permit the word at all, is on this basis to be found in the satisfaction of what Dr. Richards calls 'appetencies'. 'Anything', he says, 'is valuable which will satisfy an appetency,' provided of course that this satisfaction does not involve 'the frustration of some equal or *more important* appetency'.[1]

And if, suspecting that a value may after all be found lurking in disguise in the word 'important', we ask what is important, we are told that 'the importance of an impulse can be defined for our purposes as *the extent of the disturbance of other impulses in the individual's activities which the thwarting of the impulse involves*'.[2] This, of course, is circular, for how are we to measure 'the *extent* of the disturbance of other impulses', except by reference to the *importance* of the impulses disturbed? But this is no time to stay for mere logic. Dr. Richards is clearly in the movement. His doctrine also purports to give a meaning to beauty and goodness; it interprets art and morals in terms of the satisfaction derived from them by

[1] From Dr. Richards's *The Principles of Literary Criticism* (Chapter VII).
[2] My italics.

the individual. As for truth, we have Huxley's assertion that the best answers—by which he means, presumably, the truest answers, if he could but bring himself to use the word—'are those which permit the answerer to live most fully'. Thus truth, the object of the theoretical reason, is subordinated to, if it is not dismembered in the interests of living; and morals and the discipline of the passions, study and the life of the mind, which have been traditionally enjoined upon men by authority, reason and experience alike, are jettisoned in the interests of 'fuller' living.

II. DEFENCE OF REASON

Distinction between Theoretical and Practical Reason. The ultimate defence of reason, like the ultimate defence of philosophy, must, in my view, be related to a particular conception of the universe as a whole. This conception I have endeavoured to set forth in the second part of my *Matter, Life and Value*, and also in the concluding chapters of *Philosophical Aspects of Modern Science*. In the last two chapter of this book I shall endeavour to indicate its main features in their bearing upon the issues raised in this and the preceding chapters. My immediate concern is to examine and to try to answer the criticisms of reason which I have summarized.

Let us adopt for the purposes of discussion the distinction between the theoretical and the practical reason which the critics of reason employ. The function of the theoretical reason, we will assume, is to discover truth;

that of the practical reason, to guide our conduct, to teach us, in a word, how to live. The distinction, which is Aristotle's, prescribes an ideal, the ideal of reason's ultimate performance. For the theoretical reason the ideal is the discovery and contemplation of truth; for the practical, the right conduct of life. That reason does not think or live up to these ideals is obvious; it is obvious too that we must judge it by its actual, not its ideal, performance. How far, then, does the actual performance of reason judged in relation to these ideals, justify the contemporary strictures at which I have glanced?

Emergence of Disinterested Reasoning. It is not denied that the operations of reason in the theoretical sphere are frequently biassed by our desires and distorted by our prejudices; that we embrace conclusions not because they are true, but because we wish to think them true; and that, finding the universe as it appears unamenable to our wishes and antagonistic to our desires, we employ our reasons to persuade us that, in its real as opposed to its apparent nature, it is such as we should desire. We may even consider that most of what passes for religion and philosophy is the outcome of precisely this kind of reasoning, for which the modern world has coined the word 'rationalizing'. Does it, therefore, follow that reason can never operate freely, can never reach conclusions solely as a result of the compulsive force of the evidence?

If we look at the history of human thought, we can trace the gradual emergence of disinterested reason, and a gradual increase in the scope of its operations. Initially, it would seem, men used their reasons to justify their wishes or to further their desires, and for no other purpose at all. They certainly did not use them disinterestedly in order to acquire knowledge for its own sake.

As the mind of man develops and the employment of reason grows, a process can be discerned which the historians of human thought have traced in some detail. It is the process whereby mythology becomes religion, superstition science, alchemy chemistry, and astrology astronomy.

Let us take one or two examples of the process at work. The credit for originating it must surely belong to the Greeks. It is, indeed, their greatest achievement. Thales, travelling in the East, found that the Egyptians possessed certain rough rules of land measurement. Every year the inundation of the Nile obliterated the landmarks, and the peasants' fields had to be marked out afresh. The Egyptians had invented a method of dividing up the land into rectangular areas, by means of which they contrived to cope with the floods. Thales was not interested in marking out fields. He saw that the method could be detached from the particular purpose for which it had been used, and generalized into a method for calculating areas of any shape. So the rules of land measurement were converted into the science of geometry. The use of reason to achieve a practical end, the furtherance of human desires, had given way to the use of reason in disinterested contemplation. The disinterested contemplative reason discovered, and de-

I. Reason and Truth

lighted to discover, that the angles at the base of an isosceles triangle are always equal; discovered too why they must be equal. The land surveyor still makes use of this truth in constructing maps; reason is content to enjoy it because it is true. In the same way the Greeks turned the art of astrology into the science of astronomy. For many centuries the Babylonian priests had recorded the movements of the planets, in order to predict human events which the stars were believed to govern. The Greeks borrowed the results of their observation, and Thales predicted an eclipse which occurred in Asia Minor in 585 B.C. But they ignored the whole fabric of astrological superstition which had hitherto provided the sole, the practical motive for observing the heavens.

The movement of which Thales is so eminent an example is the beginning of science. Natural phenomena had previously been ascribed to the agency of supernatural forces. These forces had been personified into gods and devils, owning fragmentary or complete personalities accessible by prayer and sacrifice, amenable to magical compulsion, corruptible by what was known as propitiation. Thunder and lightning, for example, were the acts of these beings. It was left to Anaximander to propound the view that thunder and lightning were caused by the blast of the wind. Shut up in a thick cloud, the wind, he said, bursts forth; the tearing of the cloud makes the noise, and the rift gives the appearance of a flash in contrast with the blackness of the cloud. This is a typically *scientific* 'explanation'.

From Superstition to Science. Now it seems to me that there is an important distinction between the use of reason to persuade us that thunder and lightning are caused by beings like ourselves, who are often angry but may be propitiated, and to discover exactly how thunder and lightning are in fact caused. The former, the method of superstition, is rationalizing; it interprets the unknown in terms of the human, and arrives at explanations of phenomena which are pre-eminently gratifying, inasmuch as they represent phenomena as controllable by the human. The latter, the method of science, interprets phenomena in terms of the non-human, and propounds explanations which are ethically neutral.

It is this distinction which the wholesale disparagement of reason on the ground that it cannot be disinterested in its search for truth culpably ignores. Science has not legislated to the universe; it has been content to catalogue it. Its triumphs have been gained as the result of an impartial outlook upon the world which has sought to maintain a modest attitude towards objective fact. Instead of prescribing to things what they must be, it has been the object of the scientific method to discover what things are. It was only when science divorced itself from ethical preoccupations that it advanced. The early sciences, for example, astrology and alchemy, were dominated by utilitarian considerations. It was thought that the movements of the stars had an important influence on human beings, and that certain combinations of elements would bring untold material benefits to human lives; for these reasons the movements of the stars and the nature of the chemical combinations were studied. The early physicists were dominated by the desire to prove that the universe had a purpose and was, therefore, ethically admirable, and psychology is still to some extent influenced by the need to arrive at similar conclusions about human nature. It was only when astrology and alchemy divested themselves of utilitarian considerations, that they developed into astronomy and chemistry; only when physics emancipated itself from the need to show that the universe it studied possessed this or that ethical characteristic, that it was found possible to discover how the physical universe worked. Psychology is only now beginning to reach a certitude of result as it emancipates itself from the necessity of illustrating preconceived notions about the rationality or ethical desirability of human nature.

To reflect upon this process, the process which leads from superstition to science, as it has historically taken place, is to realize a certain highly significant fact. The victory of reason has been won first in those spheres in which both the subject matter studied and the conclusions reached are furthest removed from the sphere of the human, which are, therefore, most remote from human wishes.

Ethical Neutrality of Mathematics. The first victories are achieved in mathematics. Now, so far as I can see, the relations of numbers have no bearing whatever upon human aspirations or emotions. So far as I am concerned, seven times seven might just as well make forty-eight as forty-nine. Why, then, do I think that it makes forty-nine? Only, I imagine, because I can see that it does; at any rate, after the most careful inspection of my conscious, and a painstaking effort to acquaint myself with all that analysts tell me about my unconscious self, I can find no other reason for my belief. A poultry farmer once a week goes to market with ten dozen eggs which he sells for two pence each; he sells so many eggs every year; the up-keep of his poultry farm costs him £700 a year. How much profit does he make on every egg? I don't know; nor, I expect, does the farmer. He ought to know, you say, and he would be a more successful farmer if he did. Certainly! Therefore, you conclude, arithmetic does concern human interests. And that is where you are wrong; for the farmer's concerns are not arithmetic. They are arithmetic made easy for children by the intro-duction of a little not very successful local colouring. Arithmetic as such has not heard of farmers, has no cognizance of eggs or of the means by which they are pro-duced, and is sublimely indifferent as to whether there is a profit or not. When a problem in the arithmetic book begins. 'A poultry farmer goes to market', it is not strictly telling the truth. What it ought to say is: '*If* there were a poultry farmer who sold weekly ten dozen eggs for twopence each, and *if* the upkeep of his poultry farm cost him £700 a year, then . . . what would be the profit on each egg?' Or, more austerely still: 'What is the relation expressed in pounds, shillings and pence be-tween 120 twopences, seven hundred pounds and twelve months, in the circumstances in which . . . etc?' Arithmetic, in other words, is concerned not with facts but with relations; with the relations not between things but between quantities. No doubt the matters upon which the discovery of these relations between quantities throws light interest us enormously. Arithmetic, in fact, can be applied. It can enable us to calculate, to predict, to cheat. But the relations themselves are matters completely indifferent.

As for the fact that the product of $(a+b)$ and $(a-b)$ is a^2-b^2, I can see absolutely nothing to be said for it except that it is a fact: it is neither beautiful, holy, helpful, consoling nor useful. It just is; and mankind by a process of apparently disinterested reason has discovered that it is. It is because of its remoteness that it is in mathematics that reason first wins its triumphs, exploring the relations between numbers and mapping what it has discovered without fear or favour, and, so far as I can see, with no purpose except the desire to find out.

It is, of course, the case that even in mathematics in its early stages human wishes made their influence felt. Men anthropomorphized numbers and humanized geometrical shapes. Thus the Pythagoreans invested the number 10 with a nimbus of sanctity—it was the perfect number—and the regular pentagon with mystical significance. And all sorts of mysterious meanings have been read by cabalists into the numbers three and seven. But numbers are unsatisfactory subjects for anthropomorphization, nor is it easy to read hidden messages between the lines of an addition sum. Consequently the human element is banished quite early in civilized history from the mathematical field, and men arrive at conclusions which there is no reason for holding except that they are true. Even Aldous Huxley, so far as I know, has never been disposed to question the objective truth of mathematics, or to doubt that two and two make four, not because he wishes them to make four and has carefully chosen or cooked the evidence that favours this view, but because they do, because in fact the universe is like that.

Reason in Physics and Biology. Having acquitted itself with eminent success in mathematics, reason presently begins to invade other branches of human study, but more slowly and less surely. It is in the sciences which are remotest from human interests that the greatest measure of objectivity has been achieved, in geology, in crystallography, in chemistry and, until recently, in physics. These are the sciences which deal pre-eminently with matter and the nature of matter. It was only when physics, having whittled matter away, passed into a kind of etheric vacuum beyond it, that human aspirations in the shape of mathematically minded deities, universal mind stuff and etheric bodies, returned to fill the vacuum.

The nearer we come to the sphere of human interests, the greater the distance that separates us from objective truth. Biology is a science which, because in studying life as a whole it must needs include human life, remains still, so far as its implications are concerned, a field for conflicting theories rather than a field of ascertained facts. Biologists are continually being told that such and such is a degrading view to take, or that it is blasphemous, or that it is contrary to the truths of revealed religion. These admonitions distract them and cause them either to abandon the disliked view or to embrace it with crusading zeal. More recently they have been assured that to hold that life is an independent principle different in its intrinsic nature from matter, and that the living organism is not as a consequence adequately regarded as all body, is to make illegitimate concessions to human wishes. This view, they are told, is anthropomorphic, superstitious, sentimental, and introduces into science the unscientific myth of a mind in a machine. It is, they are admonished, a typical vice of tender-mindedness to wish to think that the mind is other than the material body, the minds of their monitors being, it is presumed, so tough as to be nothing but brains; for, if we *are* all body, our minds must, it is obvious, be our brains.

These and similar admonitions have caused the opposing creeds of mechanism and vitalism to be embraced and denied with emotional force, have made the doctrine of creative evolution into a crusade and its denial a matter of laboratory honour. They are, it is obvious, at least in part emotional in origin, the rationalizations of men's wishes, hopes, defiances and fears, and they are responsible for the limited success of biology compared with physics. It is because we want to know about life so much more than we want to know about matter, that we know so much more about matter.

The Intrusion of Wishes in Psychology and Politics. To come still nearer home to psychology, is to find the sphere of objective truth still further diminished. Psychology is not strictly speaking a science at all; it is a battle ground of conflicting theories in which Mac-Dougall controverts with Watson, Spearman with Stout, while the followers of Jung, Freud and Adler carry on a three-cornered and peculiarly embittered contest of their own. When psychology does succeed in establishing a fact, which all agree to be a fact, it turns out to be a fact not about the mind but about the body; psychology, in fact, only becomes scientific at the cost of turning into physiology. For the rest it is, and seems likely to remain, a form of myth making, whereby men supply the place of knowledge by converting their conjectures into dogmas, and then do battle on behalf of the dogmas.

As for social psychology, political theory, sociology and the other sciences, or pseudo-sciences, which study the behaviour of human beings in communities, the sciences of society, it is doubtful if even those who profess them would wish to claim on their behalf that they have entered the province of agreed, established knowledge. They are a fruitful field for speculative theories, but they touch human interests so closely, the opinions which men hold in regard to them, for example, as to whether man was made for the State or the State for man, how much we may enjoy of liberty, how much we must concede to discipline, have such a direct and momentous bearing upon human weal and woe, that it is highly unlikely that for many years to come they will enter the privileged arena in which dispassionate reason discovers and dispenses objective truth. It is, indeed, unlikely that in our civilization they ever will, the lack of the exercise of this same dispassionate reason in the communal affairs of mankind bidding fair to bring it down in ruin and catastrophe, before the lack is supplied. Some things, I should have thought, were by this time fairly obvious; that some form of democracy is the only kind of government under which minorities may be assured of a reasonable measure of toleration, individuals of justice, and that the State is an instrument for the development of the individual, not an altar for his sacrifice. But although these things are obvious to me, they seem to be diminishingly so to my contemporaries, and I may be premature in proclaiming the establishment of even these elementary truths.

Objective Truth Attainable. The conclusion of the foregoing seems to be that reason can reach objective truth; or, more precisely, the implications that underlie the process I have briefly sketched, and the assumption which the distinction between superstition and science entails are that objective truth is at least humanly attainable. Now it is, of course, the case that human beings may be wrong to draw these implications, to make this

assumption. They may be wrong, that is to say, in holding, as they undoubtedly do hold, that the methods of
astronomy are scientifically fruitful and the conclusions
of astronomers valid in some sense in which the methods
and conclusions of astrology were neither fruitful nor
valid, and that the judgment that three and two make
five is true in some sense in which the judgments that
the English are the thirteen lost tribes of Israel, or that
the great pyramid contains information as to the precise
date and manner of the destruction of the world are
not. Human minds may, I say, be wrong in drawing
these implications and in making these assumptions;
but it is certainly a fact that all intelligent human
minds, including those of Huxley, Lawrence and Richards, do draw them and do make them.

And to make them is to make also by implication the
admissions (a) that the human intellect can on occasion
discover objective fact unbiassed by prejudice and un-
distracted by desire; (b) that although it may begin by
mistaking wishes for judgments and being the dupe of
its hopes, the harder it tries and the more it develops,
the more likely it is to reach conclusions in the formation of which hopes and wishes have had no part; and
(c) that it is possible sometimes to distinguish between
those cases in which reason is functioning freely, and
those in which it is a mere puppet twitched into the
appropriate conclusions by instincts that pull the
strings. I should wish to add a fourth conclusion,
although it is more than doubtful whether the above-
mentioned writers would be willing to subscribe to it,

and, unlike the others, it does not follow from what has been said, namely, (d) that the emancipation of reason from the play of instinct and the pull of desire is a good, and that in the increase of this good lies the chief hope of our race.

This fourth conclusion is, I say, less likely to win assent. It is not so much that it is inconsistent with the explicit pronouncements of Lawrence and Huxley, of whom the former would subordinate reason to the solar plexus and the latter submerge it in life as a whole; for, so far as concerns consistency, the other three conclusions, which nobody in his senses would wish to deny, are equally at variance with some of their utterances. It is rather that in men's hearts to-day there is, I believe, a deep-seated distrust of reason and a desire to see its operations curtailed.

Reason the Prop of Social Justice. Yet apart altogether from theoretical considerations touching the advance of pure knowledge, as to whether it is a good or not that men should know things, the practical advantages of the increasing application of reason to human affairs are universally acclaimed. Consider justice, for example. Justice is a word that covers a multitude of meanings; one of them is that an innocent man should not suffer for the fault of another. Hence it is a corollary of justice that no step should be left untaken to discover the guilty. I will now suppose that a criminal lunatic, or, if you prefer, a private enemy with a grudge of malice and a taste for sadism breaks into my house, assaults my wife and slits the stomach of my baby. As soon as I who, we will suppose, am writing at the bottom of the garden, hear screams, I rush into the house but am too late to catch the lunatic sadist. I rush out into the street and see a man running at a rapid pace down the road. I catch him up and threaten him with a revolver. Hands up' I say and shout for the police, when my wife comes running up and tells me that this is the wrong man. Her assailant had lost the fore and little fingers of his right hand; the hands which are now being held up are, she observes, intact. Now the fact that I am beside myself with anger and excitement, that my emotions are violently aroused, that instinct, the instinct for revenge, that desire, the desire to capture and to punish, dominate my whole being, do not prevent my reason from operating to tell me that I have made a mistake, with the result that I lower my revolver and apologize. I am sufficiently just not to wish that an innocent man should suffer for another's crime, and it is my ability to reason that enables my sentiment of justice to take effect. Now nobody, so far as I am aware, thinks that it would be a good thing for me to attack the wrong man. I infer (a) that it is reason refusing to be biassed by instinct or desire that refuses also to allow me to give way to either; (b) that it is regarded as a good thing that reason should have achieved this degree of emancipation. The point is, indeed, so obvious that it is incredible that it should be overlooked. Yet it is, I think, quite certainly the case that it is overlooked by the writers to whom I have referred, or, more precisely, its neglect is a necessary corollary of the attitude to reason which they have both engendered and expressed. Hence, though I hesitate to labour the point, I cannot deny myself the pleasure of asking them whether, when they have every reason to believe that X, whom they loathe, has ravished their wives, and they are, therefore, thirsting for the punishment, and, unless they are eccentrically humanitarian, for the strangulation by hanging of X, they would, nevertheless, refuse to listen to the arguments of the detective who, after an elaborate accumulation of evidence, finds himself in a position to demonstrate that the murderer was not in fact X but Y, Y being uncaught and not, therefore, in immediate danger of being hung. As good readers of detective stories, in which category I confidently include both Mr. Huxley and Mr. Richards, they would, I feel sure, find themselves constrained to bow to the exegesis of the demonstrating detective. In other words, in spite of the fact that their instincts were clamouring for vengeance on X, they would obey the dictates of reason which pointed not to X but to Y. Why would they obey them? Only, so far as I can see, because of their implicit trust in the ability of reason, dispassionately considering evidence without regard to wishes, instincts or desires to reach objectively true conclusions.

Emancipation of Reason a Good. Now, I suggest again that this emancipation of reason from the predisposing bias of non-rational factors, which has resulted in the establishment of impartial justice, is a good. I think further that a similar emancipation of reason in other spheres would also be a good, and I contend that what has been achieved in logic and mathematics, is at least theoretically achievable in biology, psychology and sociology, and that it is the hope of achieving it that inspires the work of biologists, psychologists and sociologists.

Reason, emancipated from desire in mathematics has still, it is agreed, to achieve objectivity in psychology. Reason, which operates freely to reach just decisions in disputes between individuals, has still to achieve a similar objectivity in its application to disputes between nations. Already, indeed, it does on occasion operate impartially even in this sphere,[1] but the communal will to implement its deliverances is lacking. Hence the advance, which took place when astrology became astronomy and alchemy chemistry, has still to be made from the law of the jungle, based upon fear and force, which still regulates international affairs, to the law of impartial justice administered by disinterested parties, which already prevails in disputes between individuals.

Truth and Verifiability. There is a further application of these conclusions. The school of thought I have described is, as we have seen in previous essays, scornful of philosophy and religion. Both, it holds, are forms of wish fulfilment, projections of the desires of the human

[1] E.g. in the admirable pronouncements of the Bank for International Settlements or the International Labour Office.

heart or the fantasies of the human mind upon the empty canvas of the universe. Neither can claim truth. It is not my intention here to defend philosophy, which is later to be accorded a couple of chapters in its exclusive honour. It is sufficient for my purpose to point out that, if I am right in supposing that the achievement of objective truth by the human mind is at last possible in other spheres, there is no reason why it should be impossible in those of philosophy and religion.

The difference between astronomy or geology, let us say, and philosophy is not a difference between spheres in which truth is possible and achievable and a sphere in which it is not; it is a difference between spheres in which truth *can be known* to have been achieved and one in which no such knowledge is possible. The difference between the conclusions of science and of philosophy is, in a word, not one of truth but of verifiability. If I believe that the attraction between two bodies varies inversely with the square of the distance between them, I can by means of suitable apparatus establish the fact that my belief is correct. If I believe with Bradley that judgment is an act which ascribes an ideal content to reality, there is no available means of verification which will tell me whether my belief is correct or not. But it does not, therefore, follow that it cannot be correct; nor does it follow in the case of judgments of value.

If five people are asked to guess the temperature of a room, two things will happen: first, they will all guess differently; secondly, their estimates will be relative to and determined by subjective, physiological conditions prevailing in themselves. It does not follow, however, that the room has not got a temperature. What is more, we can by using a thermometer find out what it is; we can also find out which of the guesses is nearest the truth. Similarly, if five people are asked to pronounce upon the æsthetic value of a picture, or a quartet, it is probable that all will estimate it differently; moreover, the varying estimates will be relative to and determined by subjective circumstances of training, environment and taste, that is, by the æsthetic experience, the age and culture of the judges. It does not, therefore, follow either that the work of art has no æsthetic value in its own right, or that some of the judgments will not be nearer the mark than others. The only difference from the preceding instance is that in the present case there is no instrument analogous to the thermometer, by reference to which we can test the respective accuracies of the differing judgments. It is for this reason that art criticism is a battle of *ipse-dixitisms* and that there is no disputing about anything but tastes.

Conclusions. I conclude, then, first, that reason can sometimes reach results which are objectively and absolutely true. This is notably the case in the sphere of mathematics; it is frequently the case in that of the sciences; it is also the case in human affairs in the degree to which we are prepared to hang a man who is rich and respected by eminent persons in preference to one who is poor and a known Communist, merely because the evidence shows that he and not the Com-

I. Reason and Truth

munist committed the crime. Secondly, that this capacity
of reason is in practice recognized by those whose doctrine requires them to deny it, since they no more doubt
that three and two make five and that a man ought to
be and sometimes is hanged in accordance with evidence
and not political prejudice or personal dislike, than I
do. Thirdly, that we can trace as a historical process the
spread of reason and its gradual invasion of new spheres.
Fourthly, that in its success in bringing under its ægis
spheres which have hitherto been the province of emotion and feeling lies the chief hope of the race.

Chapter VI

Defence of Reason—II. Reason and Conduct

★

Thinking as the Enemy of Living. Huxley's ideal of conduct is, it is clear, the Greek. He sings the praises of a balanced living in which every side of man's nature gets a square deal. 'The art of life', he reminds us, 'consisted for them [the Greeks] in giving every god his due. These dues were various. Thus, Apollo's due was very different from the debt a man owed to Dionysus . . . but everyone was owed, and, in its proper time and season, must be acknowledged. No god must be cheated and none overpaid.' A man's duty is, then, to acknowledge *all* the gods, to neglect none. Doing our duty we 'make the best of the world and its loveliness while we can—at any rate during the years of youth and strength'.

Now this ideal is, we are explicitly told, incompatible with overmuch thinking. For reason, unless it is checked, will inhibit the use of the other faculties, preying like a cancer upon the organism as a whole. And not only reason, but conscience, will, foresight—in fact all man's most conscious and most lately evolved faculties. 'Circumstances', Huxley complains, 'have led humanity to set an ever-increasing premium on the conscious and intellectual comprehension of things. Modern man's besetting temptation is to sacrifice his direct perceptions and spontaneous feelings to his reasoned reflections; to prefer in all circumstances the verdict of his intellect to that of his immediate intuitions. "L'homme est visiblement fait pour penser," says Pascal; "c'est toute sa dignité, et tout son mérite et tout son devoir est de penser comme il faut." Noble words; but do they happen to be true? Pascal seems to forget that man has something else to do besides think: he must live.'

As I hinted in the preceding essay, the profounder answer to this view, the view that reason is the enemy of life and that it must, therefore, be chastened in the interests of fuller living, lies in the affirmation of a positive metaphysic, the lines of which I shall endeavour briefly to indicate in two final chapters. My present business is that of examination and criticism which, meeting the Huxleyan philosophy at its own level of popular moralizing, seeks to challenge its adequacy on that level.

Greek Life not Instinctive. Let us, then, accept, with the proviso that a profounder view may reveal grounds for qualifying our complete acceptance, the doctrine that the best life is the fullest. The word 'fullest' we will further interpret in Huxley's sense—which is also for the greater part of his *Ethics* Aristotle's sense—as denoting the completest development of all our faculties, the most various activity of every aspect of our being, instinctive as well as intellectual, unconscious as well as conscious.

Can such a life be described as instinctive? Obviously it cannot. On the contrary, it can only be pursued by virtue of the continuous and unremitting vigilance of the practical reason. An analogy of Plato's will help to demonstrate the point. He likens the human personality to a chariot drawn by a number of unruly horses. Each horse wants to follow a different course and tries to pull the chariot in a different direction from the other horses. Left to themselves, therefore, the divergent pulls of the horses would neutralize one another and bring the chariot to a standstill, or, if one horse were to prove suddenly stronger than the others, he would dash it to pieces against the first obstacle that stood in its way. At best the chariot would pursue a guideless, aimless course zigzagging hither and thither and failing to reach any specified goal. But in addition to the horses, there is, says Plato, the charioteer who holds the reins and controls and guides them. This he does, not by frustrating all the desires of all the horses, but by allowing to each one only so much of its way as is compatible with the humouring of the others. What in fact the charioteer does is to see fair play; and fair play means dovetailing the wills of the various horses into some sort of unity, and directing the chariot along a line which is the resultant of all their separate pulls. This line the chariot can consistently maintain, and reach whatever objective it is aiming at. Thanks, then, to the charioteer, there is substituted for an aimless zigzag course, liable at any moment to the risk of sudden disaster, a consistent progress in a preconceived direction. Read 'separate desires and impulses' for 'horses', and 'reason' for 'charioteer', and the analogy illustrates well enough the point I wish to bring out.

And the point is this. If you are to have a full and reasonably balanced life, a life which assigns proper satisfaction to each of your various impulses and desires, you must put reason in control. Now Huxley does at times betray a glimmering apprehension of this truth. In the concluding paragraphs of one of his books of essays, throughout the whole course of which the life of reason has been disparaged in the interests of life *tout court*, he concedes: 'And yet the life worshipper is also, in his own way, a man of principles and consistency. To live intensely—that is his guiding principle. His diversity is a sign that he consistently tries to live up to his principles.' But this admission gives the game away. For how is consistency to be achieved, how are principles to be observed, except by the constant vigilance, the unremitting exercise of reason? To subject one's impulses and desires to reason is not to frustrate them; it is merely to prevent any group of them from running away with you and denying satisfaction to the rest.

The Calculated Restraint of Impulse. The point is so obvious that I hesitate to labour it. Yet it is also so frequently ignored that I must be pardoned, if I resort to one or two simple illustrations to drive it home. When I climb a mountain, I am continuously solicited by an impulse to turn round and look at the view. Now experience has taught me that I get most enjoyment, if I restrain this impulse until I have reached the top. I then allow the view to break upon me in all its fullness, its freshness unimpaired by surrender to the temptation to contemplate its inadequate revelation. The impulse to enjoy the scenery is not frustrated by rationally imposed restraint; on the contrary, reason by guarding it against premature fulfilment, has secured its maximum satisfaction.

Smoking. Like most male adults I have an impulse to smoke cigarettes. This impulse was not part of my initial equipment. As with most of our tastes that are both permanent and valuable, the taste for smoking is acquired. At first I smoked on principle, the principle that it is always worth cultivating a new want in order to enjoy the pleasure of satisfying it. The want established, every cigarette was for a time a pleasure. Presently, however, the appetite for cigarettes, growing with what it fed on, began to demand more frequent satisfactions, so much so, that in course of time it came to dominate my youthful consciousness. By this time I was sensible of a definite feeling of discomfort whenever I was not smoking. Accordingly, I smoked the more in order to allay this feeling of discomfort. I did not now derive any positive pleasure from smoking; I smoked as an unconscious habit to satisfy an ever-present need. The need grew ever more insistent, until I could not bear to be without a cigarette between my lips. At this point reason stepped in and insisted on being heard.

II. Reason and Conduct

Reason pointed out that whereas previously I had smoked to get pleasure, I now smoked to allay discomfort. The state of smoking was now hedonically neutral; it was neither pleasant nor painful; but the state of not smoking was definitely a pain. Thus I was expending an ever-increasing quantity of time, energy and money in order to derive an ever-diminishing quantity of satisfaction. By God's grace I listened to reason. I do not now smoke cigarettes; I smoke the more easily regulated pipe. I smoke four pipes a day; rarely more, never less. Each is looked forward to with pleasure; each confers pleasure. My first pipe occurs after lunch, the others after dinner. There is no craving in the morning; there is no craving after tea. Thus not only is my pleasure as a whole sensibly increased, but the desire to smoke, guided and controlled by reason, has been exploited in such a way as to confer its maximum of satisfaction.

Bathing before Breakfast. I have an impulse to bathe before breakfast on a fine summer morning. It is an impulse which I find it difficult to resist. I have however found by experience that, if I yield to it, my morning's work is ruined. I am hot-eyed and stupid at ten, desperately sleepy at eleven; by twelve I have given up the struggle and subsided into a splenetic novel, probably one of Huxley's. If I resist the impulse and postpone my bathe until the middle of the afternoon, none of these things happens to me. My head remains clear; I do a reasonable morning's work: I refrain from reading Aldous Huxley. What is more, I get a better bathe. In the early morning my vitality is low, my powers of enjoyment below par. Consequently, for all its apparent seduction, I always enjoy a bathe before breakfast less than I expect to. In the afternoon I invariably enjoy it more.

Drinking before Speech Making. Before addressing a meeting I experience a strong impulse to have a drink. A glass of sherry, or, better still, a cocktail, will, I feel, remove nervousness and increase alertness; it will put a kick into my sentences, a polish on my style and a point into my witticisms. In fact it does none of these things. On the contrary it clouds my mind and addles my wits. I can't think of the right things to say and I can't think of the right words to say them in. I can neither imagine facts with which to answer, nor devise anecdotes with which to divert, the awkward questioner. And, having learnt these things by bitter experience, I drink coffee before a speech and refrain from intoxicants until after-wards, when I enjoy them all the better for bringing to them an already excited mood. But I have no *impulse* to drink coffee.

Reason Necessary for Enlightened Hedonism. There are, no doubt, perfectly good physiological causes for these effects. To take a bathe on an empty stomach is to take exercise with a system unfortified by glucose and carbo-hydrates. Carbohydrates act as a screen to the proteins in the body, a buffer which stands between them and the full blast of its activity. Lacking the protection of the carbohydrates, the proteins break down. In so doing they release acid into the blood stream, a circumstance which accounts for the faintness and fatigue felt by those who exercise unfed.

Alcohol, it is well known, increases the reaction time of the nervous centres in the brain, slowing down their rate of vibration as one mutes the strings of a violin. And so on. . . . What do these physiological facts indicate? To put it brutally, that we often have impulses to do what is bad for us. How salutary, then, to check them by reason in the interests of one's total good. And not only of one's total good, but also of their own. I get more pleasure from the view, more enjoyment from my pipe; I have a better bathe, make a better speech, and get more kick out of my subsequent drink, because reason has taught me not to obey the impulse to look at the view, to smoke, to bathe and to drink when it is first felt. Hence, to practise that very doctrine of hedonism that bids us make pleasure our end in order that we may derive the fullest and the most varied sensations from being alive, it is necessary to place reason in control, since to check impulse by reason is often to increase one's enjoyment of that for which the impulse is felt.

Ability to reason accurately is, indeed, essential to living properly, for by accurate reasoning alone can we calculate our actions, so as to do what we intend to do; that is to fulfil our will.

As it is with view appreciating and smoking and bathing and speech making, so it is with the more important, the more clamant impulses. I have deliberately taken instances of impulses which are neither very strong nor very primitive. To transfer the argument to the major impulses, the impulses to food and sex and self-preservation, is to reinforce its conclusion. To let one's appetite for food run away with one is to become a gourmand, vainly trying to extract pleasure from new dishes with which one's lack of appetite renders one increasingly critical. To obey every sexual impulse is to render oneself in the end incapable of sex satisfaction. To seek to preserve oneself by unprepared attack upon an enemy directly one sees him, or by flight directly he sees one, is to rush upon destruction. It is better to ambush before attacking; to turn suddenly at bay in the midst of apparently incontinent flight.

Our race, in fact, owes such civilization as it has achieved to its ability to restrain its impulses, in order to secure their more effective gratification. The point I am making is, I repeat, so obvious that I feel compunction in ramming it home. Rammed home, however, it must be, and unable any longer to tolerate the sight and sound of my own words conveying platitudes whose obvious truth, when first announced by Aristotle, should have precluded the need for their restatement once and for all, I propose to invoke Bishop Butler to be platitudinous for me.

Bishop Butler on Cool Self-Love. Butler is an admirable psychologist, who almost succeeds in performing that most difficult of philosophical feats, the feat of making righteousness readable. The outstanding feature of his ethics is the distinction between the separate self-regarding impulses, Plato's chariot horses, and what he calls 'cool self-love'. Cool self-love is a man's general desire for the good of the whole, that is for his good as a whole. It is cool self-love which prompts a man to seek his own maximum happiness over the whole course of his life. If the object of self-love is happiness, that of the particular passions is far otherwise. In the case of hunger or of avarice it is easy to see that this is so. But just as the object of hunger is food, and of avarice wealth, so the object of boasting—and who shall deny the impulse to boast?—is to increase the estimation in which one is held by one's hearers, of malice to do somebody an injury, of anger to do anybody or anything an injury, even if it is only the furniture.

Now it is pretty clear that many of the particular passions and impulses conflict with cool self-love. Although my object in boasting is to cause others to fear or to admire me, in fact my boasts usually evoke the opposite sentiments, a result which in course of time becomes so patently, so regrettably clear, that most of us cease to boast except when drunk, drunkenness being a condition in which the inhibitions imposed by cool self-love upon the various impulses and passions are weakened. If I break the furniture in a rage, it is almost certain that I shall have to pay for it afterwards; if in a passion of instinctive repugnance I bash the face of a sandy-haired man wearing a panama hat, I shall almost certainly be summoned for assault. Cool self-love is, then, not only different from but frequently antagonistic to the particular passions. When such antagonism arises, the victory of cool self-love is likely to increase one's total happiness.

Social Desirability of Enlightened Selfishness. And not only one's own total happiness, but that of the world. If people were to act consistently according to the dictates of self-love, their actions would not, Butler points out, be very different from those which they would perform, if they acted consistently from the principle of benevolence. By acting in such a way as to promote our own real good, we almost always promote the good of others, and vice versa. When we believe that we shall do good to ourselves by harming others, it will be found that the belief is almost always false.

It is this belief that usually accompanies the indulgence of the particular passions. Indulging the passion for vengeance, we inflict financial ruin or gross physical suffering on somebody we believe to have done us an injury. But, even if we escape the normal penalties of violence by squaring the police, or contriving to live under a dictatorship which confers upon its supporters the prerogative of taking vengeance with impunity upon those whom they conceive to have 'wronged' them by venturing to disagree with their opinions, the personal gratifications of vengeance are notoriously unsatisfying. I say 'notoriously' because, owing to a preponderance of cool self-love, I cannot remember myself to have taken vengeance upon anybody in recent years. I accordingly accept the opinion of poets and moralists and the testimony of most murderers and torturers, which is almost unanimous on the subject.

Similarly with regard to malice, which may be described as a disinterested desire for somebody else's discomfiture. The policy pursued by France towards Germany in the years immediately succeeding the war owed its inspiration in almost equal degrees to malice and the desire for vengeance. The results show how much better it would have been for the French to have been guided by cool self-love. Germany, maddened by the rejection of all her overtures for a sympathetic understanding and outraged by the continual breaking on the part of others of pledges which she had been compelled to observe, has developed a militant intransigence which the French do right to fear. But having deliberately maddened Germany over a period of years, it is a little disingenuous, to say the least of it, on the part of her tormentors to complain because they discern foam on her lips. If the French had pursued a policy of enlightened self-interest, instead of acting from mingled motives of malice, vengeance and fear, not only they and the Germans but the Western world as a whole would now be calmer, saner and happier.

In general I believe it to be the case that those actions which are the most hurtful to others, are never those which a man who aimed at the maximum happiness for himself would perform. The contrary is also true. If men acted rationally, that is to say, in the way which was most likely to bring about the ends they desire, Utopia would be realized. But most men are actuated by impulses and passions which cloud their judgment and persuade them that by injuring those whom they fear or dislike they will advantage themselves. It is one of the paradoxes of human conduct that men do not, as a general rule, act in a way which is calculated to advance their own interest from rational motives, although self-interest is one of the objects of rational desire. It is only when they are actuated by generous motives, which as a rule are indifferent to their own interest, that they in fact advance it. The paradox arises from the fact that those actions which are likely to promote the maximum happiness of the self are usually identical with those which will be likely to benefit others; or, as Butler would saÿ, actions dictated respectively by the promptings of cool self-love and benevolence tend to be identical, a fact which may or may not be evidence for the conclusions that God exists, that He created the world, that there is an underlying harmony in things, and that human society, in spite of all the evidence to the contrary, is founded on ethical principles.

Subordination of Impulses to Cool ‘Self-Love. This much at least seems to be fairly certain, that it is in the domination of the various impulses and passions by cool self-love that the chief hope of happiness for the individual lies. In other words, the happy life is not the instinctive life, in which without rule or principle, system or plan, we gratify each and every aspect of our personality, as it happens to come uppermost at the moment, but a life in which the various passions are duly subordinated to

rational control in the interests of coherent and purposive living. Now coherent and purposive living will
include among its objects, although it will not acknowledge as its only object, the achievement of the maximum possible happiness for the individual.

The preceding analysis, for the length of which I
apologize, has been undertaken in the interests of the
practical reason. It has been my object to show that, so
far from being hostile to life, as Huxley avers, the practical reason enables us to live it more fully; that so far
from being the enemy of the passions, it guarantees their
fulfilment. But it can do this, only if it restrains them.
The function of reason in this connection is twofold. It
must keep the ring in the interests of all the passions,
and must from time to time chastise each of them in the
interests of itself. It must, that is to say, restrain passion
A, both in order to give fair play to passions B, C and D;
and also because, by taking the bit between its teeth,
passion A may, like a runaway horse, become the enemy
of its own gratification.

Fallacy of 'The Good Time'. No passion, it is obvious,
can be gratified all the time; what is not perhaps so
obvious is that it must not in its own interests be gratified as often as it demands. We cannot, in fact, feast
unless we are prepared also to fast. That this should be
so may be, no doubt is, regrettable; but the boredom of
the sensualist, the drugtaker and the pleasure addict
proves to demonstration that it is so. One of the great
catches of life, in short, is that unrestricted hedonism

does not work. Huxley knows this well enough; nobody, in fact, has exposed more devastatingly the wretchedness of the perpetual 'good time'. What he does not seem to realize is that the practical outcome of his vendetta against the practical reason as the guide and chastener of the passions, is to leave us with no alternative to the 'good time'.

Definition of the Rational Man. In general a rational man may be defined as one who allows himself to be influenced by considerations which are not immediately relevant. The definition refers only to reason in its relation to conduct, and in relation to conduct the role it assigns to reason is such as man's evolutionary history would lead us to expect. For in what respect does man chiefly differ from the animals? In respect of his ability to be stimulated to activity by objects not immediately present to his senses. The dog is stimulated by present smells, scarcely, if at all, by the remembrance of past ones; the cat knows only that fish is not *now* in the cupboard; he cannot comfort himself with the thought that to-morrow is Friday. Now man, unlike the dog and the cat, possesses the faculty of imagination. He can think of objects and events with which he has no immediate physical relation, of objects remote in space, of events remote in time. His activity here and now may be, and often is, determined by reference to such objects. It is precisely because of this ability to enter into cognitive relations with the not sensuously present, that man has been able to evolve art, science, mathematics, politics, government. And not unnaturally he prides himself upon it, knowing it to be the distinguishing characteristic of his species.

It is not, then, matter for surprise that the possession of a greater or less degree of this ability should chiefly differentiate men from men. The more of it we possess, the more completely human do we become. My children dislike going to bed because, sensible only of the pleasure of to-night, they forget to-morrow's fatigue. I, more rational, point out that we have a long journey in front of us, and that unless we want to be wretched all day, we had better go to bed now. My advice takes account of considerations not immediately relevant; it exhibits me, therefore, as more rational than my children. It is also in the long run more productive of pleasure. In fact the main reason why the rational man permits himself to be influenced by factors not present to his senses, is his discovery that by this method he will derive from life the maximum pleasure. Perpetually, therefore, he takes thought for to-morrow, and forgoes some of the more obvious satisfactions of the moment in the interests of greater satisfaction to come. The man who resists an offer of good port after lunch because he knows that he will have to use his brains in the afternoon, the man who in spite of strong provocation remains sexually abstinent on the night preceding a tennis match, the boat race or an ascent of Mount Everest, the man who, fearing sleeplessness, resists his curiosity to open an important letter at night knowing that he will bring to it a fresher and less excitable mind in the morning; even the Christian

who forgoes the more obvious pleasures now, and deliberately submits to a little wholesome boredom on
Sundays in the belief that by forgoing and submitting he
will enjoy more quintessential pleasures in perpetuity
hereafter—all these are employing reason in order to
secure for themselves the opportunity for fuller and more
varied living, although the last would do well to scrutin-
ize closely the credentials of the belief, on the basis of
which alone his somewhat hazardous restraints are
justified. (How sold he would be, if he found that there
was no hereafter, or that the qualifications so laboriously
acquired were the wrong ones.)

The Intellect too has its Claims. Two subsidiary matters
remain, and my defence is finished. We are, it will be
remembered, bidden by Huxley to develop every side
of our being, to live out to the full extent of all our
faculties. We must not, he warns us, allow our lives to be
ridden by the hag consistency; for life is not consistent.
We are not one man, but many; not a personal unit, but
a bundle of persons. Very well, then, he concludes, let
us live as variously as our natures are various; let us be
ascetics to-day, sensualists to-morrow; let us be students
in the morning, rakes in the evening; let us worship God
on Sunday and Mammon all the week. Let us, in fact,
'give every God his due'.

So be it! But is not Athena also a God, or rather a
Goddess? Do not men among their other faculties also
possess reason, possess it, indeed, so thoroughly that to
reason is with many of us, including Huxley himself,

second nature. Consider, for example, that human activity known as the disinterested pursuit of knowledge for its own sake. Men strive with little prospect of success to comprehend the nature of the universe as a whole; they strive with little hope of reward to find out how it works in detail. Many men, and they are not by the suffrages of their kind deemed the most ignoble, have given their lives to these pursuits. Why? One may answer, if one is addicted to the terminology of impulse, because they are impelled by the impulse of curiosity; or, if you prefer it, by the impulse to reason. I suspect that we are but playing with words here. The precise psychological machinery that we invoke to account for the fact that we positively do use our reasons for their own sweet sakes, is unimportant. The fact is that we do perpetually so use them without any inducement of money or fame or material reward, for the sheer fun of the thing. And the more civilized we are, the more we are apt to do it; the more, that is to say, we are apt to employ our reasons about matters which do not directly concern us. Culture, indeed, is, I have suggested, essentially a preoccupation with matters which do not directly concern us and cannot possibly conduce to our advantage. Why, then, in the interests of the full and varied life which Huxley commends, should we forgo the exercise of this disinterested activity which is, to put it at its lowest, by no means the least interesting of our faculties?

But it is not only in the pursuit of abstract knowledge that the disinterested reason is exercised. Men have, and women have especially, a disposition disinterestedly to observe their neighbours; they catalogue and comment upon their idiosyncrasies and base generalizations with regard to the species as a whole upon the behaviour of the specimens catalogued. Huxley excells at this activity; it constitutes, indeed, if we are to judge from his writings, the major interest of his life. Yet it is an activity pre-eminently rational.

The activity of reason, in fact, is not only an integral part of full and various living. It becomes, as man grows more civilized, a necessary part. Why deny the fact, or why, if you admit it, deplore it?

Exciting Lives of the Philosophers. Secondly, I would ask, is it in any sense true that those who have lived what is popularly known as the life of the mind, have been guilty of the passional, emotional and æsthetic starvation which Huxley castigates? Applied to the lives of some of the great philosophers of the past, there may be some substance in his charge. Kant, for example, appears to have erected the terrific edifice of his moral philosophy upon a very exiguous foundation of moral experience; should he, or should he not permit himself another sweet cake at tea? He never could decide the point satisfactorily. The temptation was great, but he was growing fat and the indulgence was, he knew, not good for him. From the moral struggles that ensued the Categorical Imperative was born. Kant, then, affords a possible example of the life atrophied by intellect. But in this as in other respects he was an exceptional philosopher.

II. Reason and Conduct

In point of varied and exciting experience the lives of most of the great philosophers put those of my students, who casually cite the 'mutilated' existences of great thinkers as testimonies to the atrophying effects of the intellect, completely in the shade. Socrates being murdred; Plato trying to bring up a young tyrant at Syracuse and getting sacked for his pains; Aristotle tutoring Alexander the Great; Spinoza being expelled from the Jewish community for atheism; Hume acting as secretary to the English Ambassador to France and becoming the lion of eighteenth-century Parisian society; Descartes serving as a soldier in the Low Countries, fighting for the Duke of Bavaria on the Danube, getting into trouble with the Church for the *Discourse on Method*, going for years in terror of the fate of Galileo, and finally dying of inflammation of the lungs through getting up at five in the morning to teach the Queen of Sweden philosophy, lived lives which for sheer interest and excitement exhibit the existences of a clerk, a University undergraduate or an Aldous Huxley as cowlike browsings in the meadows of vapid uneventfulness.

'Intellectuals' as Bad Mixers and Bad Consumers. So much for the great philosophers. Consider next the contemporary 'intellectual'. He is distinguished by two negative characteristics, both of which Huxley is careful to point out. First, he shares Huxley's horror of 'the good time'. He does not listen to 'crooners', respond with sympathy to the sounds proceeding from American larynxes at the 'talkies', indulge in the stilted perambulations

slightly impeded by a member of the opposite sex which is known as modern dancing. He does not go to see horses competing at Ascot, or men perfecting themselves in the contemporary arts of efficient killing by dropping bombs from aeroplanes at Hendon, or reproducing those of the past by charging on horses at the Aldershot tattoo. He does not rotate on roundabouts on Hampstead Heath on Bank Holidays, or lounge moodily or hilariously on the beach at Margate or Blackpool. In short, he goes his own way and avoids the crowd.

Secondly, he is, as I have already noted, an extraordinarily bad consumer: he does not need a wireless; he is content not to possess a car; he is not 'maty', and does not, therefore, spend his evenings swapping drinks with cronies in a pub. He is generally bad at games, and has been so firmly 'conditioned' against them by his experiences at a public school, that he has lost any inclination he might have had to identify the good life with the whacking of round bits of matter with long thin ones; he tends accordingly to be without bats, mallets, racquets, clubs, hockey sticks or cues. He is congenitally incapable of operating gadgets and, because of the feeling of inferiority his incapacity gives him, refuses to possess them. He does not take delight in his clothes, bedew himself with hair oil, or attach to his fingers, ties or cuffs pieces of shining stone and metal. He has a simple toothpaste and does not change it; and, as often as not, he grows a beard and does not shave. Hence, as Huxley has himself suggested, the deliberate modern cult of 'lowbrowism' as a direct reprisal on the part of producers for the low 'highbrow' consumption of goods.

Pursuits and Praise of the 'Intellectual'. What, then, is the 'highbrow' doing when he is resisting the blandishments of jazz, failing to drive in cars, to own vacuum cleaners or to thrill at the 'movies'? He is reading, or walking in the country; that is to say his consumption is limited to shoe-leather, books and beer; in extreme cases he is on his back content with 'a green thought in a green shade', that is to say, he is not consuming at all. Further, he may bathe, climb—he is given to climbing—ride horses, a pursuit to which when reasonably well off he has recently become addicted, skate, ski, travel, explore, play chess. If, in spite of his public school training, he can still tolerate games, he will be found playing them rather than watching them.

Pursuits and Dispraise of the 'Lowbrow'. Now compare these pursuits by and large with the pursuits of the 'lowbrow'. While the former involve a more or less continuous expenditure of energy, skill and intelligence, the latter are creation saving, energy economizing, thought atrophying. They demand no effort, no exercise, no talent; summon no faculty of mind or body to its full activity. Untrained and undeveloped, slack and fat, sleepy and bored, the 'lowbrows' ride in cars, sit in cafés and cinemas, drink in pubs, lounge on beaches, 'enjoying' the standardized pleasures which it pays somebody to provide for them.

The 'Intellectual' Returns to Nature

With senses alert, with nerves taut, with every fibre of their physical being quivering with excited life, the 'highbrows' climb, ride, ski, yacht, explore deserts, discover planets or split atoms. Reading poetry, enjoying a sunset, enraptured by a view, savouring the smells of dawn on a spring morning or of dusk on an autumn evening, or listening with all the passion of the responding soul to the music of Bach, they cultivate the arduous joys of the spirit. Playing chess, reading philosophy, maintaining a thesis, pleading a cause, following or joining in cultivated talk, they exercise the mind. To whom, then, are we to give the palm for full and varied living so justly praised by Huxley? The answer is clear: it must be to the 'intellectual', to the man who, refusing to yield up all his being to the impulses of the moment or to allow his tastes and pursuits to be dictated by the purveyors of consumable goods, determines his life by a reasoned appraisement of the things that seem to him to be good.

The 'Intellectual' Returns to Nature. Even by those quaint Lawrencian standards, the submerging of the spirit in the dark heart of things, the vibrating in harmony with the rhythms of the universe, the pulsing with the beats of cosmic being, the drawing of strength and inspiration from the fount of nature—even by these standards (always assuming that these expressions of Lawrence's have some meaning, and that the only conceivable meaning that I can think of for them is the sort of meaning Lawrence intended them to bear) the 'intellectual' gets marks; indeed, he tops the whole class of his contemporaries.

In the modern world it is the 'intellectual who camps, hikes, sleeps out of doors, goes for midnight tramps, gazes at sunsets and the stars, feeds on grass and vegetables. It is also the intellectual who, having deliberately inflamed his imagination by the reading of poetry, burns as a youth with romantic love, as a young man in Bloomsbury or Chelsea enjoys his succession of mistresses, and even in middle age indulges in occasional extra-marital 'affairs' with more facility and gusto and far less shame and compunction than his 'lowbrow' contemporary smirking and guffawing over his dirty stories in the club smoking-room. Whether this communing with nature, this richer and more varied sex life are to the point, I do not know. The trouble with 'life worship' is that it is so difficult to reduce to concrete terms, so hard to find out precisely what it 'comes to' in practice. But I take it that, at least in Lawrence's view, 'the great, dark blood stream' which surges in the abdomen and the guts demands an outlet through the channels of sex. It is, indeed, from the loins that the 'deep gusts' of the spirit chiefly blow, if one may judge from Lawrence's own works, and a proper outlet for these gusts would, accordingly, seem to require a substantial degree of varied and passionate sex life. I conclude, therefore, that even from this point of view, the intellectual, that is to say the man who finds in the arts and the sciences, philosophy, mathematics, sociology or even politics his main interest and activity and, while functioning primarily on the intellectual plane, is yet notoriously lax in his morals, gets marks over his 'lowbrow' competitor.

Leisure of 'Intellectuals' and of Business Men. When I compare the way in which I am spending my leisure this hot summer at ——, reading and writing all the morning, sleeping after lunch, playing tennis or sometimes cricket in the afternoon, bathing in the Arun, fishing for pike from a punt on the lake or riding on the downs in the cool of the evening, bathing perhaps again by moonlight and rounding off the day by singing in chorus in the inn or a little poetry read aloud before bed—when, I say, I compare the activities of an average intellectual trying to enjoy his holiday and succeeding, with those of the average business or professional man whom I see lounging on the beach at Littlehampton, riding on a switchback, watching games that he never plays, listening to songs he does not sing, betting on horses that he never rides, going in the evening with his wife to the cinema to smack his lips over the female beauty that he never enjoys, drinking whiskies in the lounge of a hotel, sitting hour after hour at contract bridge, dancing a little and then again drinking, having in fact gloriously but determinedly 'a good time', it seems to me that, judged by the very standards which Huxley, Lawrence and the anti-intellectualist school set up, it is I who am living the right life, the business man who lives the wrong one.

Yet, if my way of life were to win the Huxley-Law-

II. Reason and Conduct

rence prize, as I hope it may, I cannot forbear to point out that its conduct depends largely upon the constant operation of two factors, at both of which the examiners look askance. First, the whole of my morning is dedicated shamelessly to the uses of the intellect. Until lunch time I read and write philosophy, and I do this in pursuance of a quite deliberate plan. I find that work is the only occupation I can stand in any but the smallest of doses, and that, if I give up the whole of my day to amusing myself, even if my amusements are of the approved Huxley-Lawrence type, I only succeed in boring myself. Secondly, the activities of the rest of the day are carefully planned and deliberately varied on two principles. First, I consider some activities such as the reading of poetry, the singing of songs and the enjoyment of nature, to be good in themselves.[1] They are, therefore, followed for their own sake. Secondly, I agree with Huxley that I must try to give every side of my nature a fair show. I must, that is to say, employ as many of my faculties as possible and vary their employment as much as possible. Now both these are principles laid down for me by reason.

[1] The sense in which I use 'good in themselves' was explained in a previous chapter. See pages 68, 69.

Chapter VII

Defence of Philosophy—I. Philosophy and Life

★

Reason having, I trust, been vindicated, I come at last to my official defence of philosophy. That philosophy has an important effect upon life I am convinced. This effect is, however, not a direct one, nor is it one which it is easy to describe.

By saying that the effect of philosophy is not direct, I mean that, unlike religion, philosophy does not exhort us to lead one kind of life rather than another; it has, in other words, no specific message. It is, nevertheless, a fact that one who has been engaged in the study of philosophical problems for a period of, say, two or three years, will find that his outlook on life is profoundly different from what it was when the study began. The difference, however, will have no very obvious relation to the problems studied, nor is it easy to say in what it consists. I want, nevertheless, in this chapter to try to indicate as briefly as I can what sort of effect philosophy has upon those who study it, why it is valuable and how it is produced.

Unfounded Claims for Philosophy.　It will be well

I. Philosophy and Life

to begin by specifying the things that philosophy will *not* do for us, in order that we may not be led to entertain false expectations of the benefits that attend its study. Philosophy will not help us to enlarge our incomes, to become social successes, to increase the effectiveness of our personalities, or our popularity among our friends. It may even do the reverse of these things. And, since most people to-day assess the value of a study by the standard of its concrete results in terms of worldly success, philosophy tends to be under a cloud. Threatened on one side by the spread of popular science and on the other by the encroachments of psychology, it stands low in popular favour, and tends to be impatiently dismissed as an idle exercise in word spinning. In particular it is said that philosophy has no relationship to life, and that it has arrived at no definite and generally agreed results.

Let us consider each of these charges separately. If by the first is meant that philosophy does not solve for us the practical problems of everyday existence, the charge must be admitted. If life is an art, philosophers are not its artists, nor does the study of philosophy confer a knowledge of its technique. If life be regarded as a chess problem, philosophy does not provide a ready-made solution; while, in so far as philosophers have claimed that the study of their works fitted the student for the business of life, the claim is largely unfounded. That a knowledge of philosophy does not directly affect the business of living, an observation of philosophers will readily prove. The political philosopher is not noticeably better either as a citizen or as a statesman than his neighbour. The metaphysician cannot provide an agreed and demonstrably correct answer to the questions, how the universe started, whether it works mechanically, whether there is a God, or whether there is matter. The morals of the ethical philosopher are not markedly superior to those of the plain man. In particular he is not necessarily remarkable for what is known as the 'philosophic temperament'. He is no more serene and he is not better tempered than the man in the street, being just as likely to betray ill temper when he breaks a bootlace, or to swear when he misses his train. A knowledge of all the ethical systems that have been propounded since man began to moralize will not make the philosopher a good man, and thinking will certainly not make him a happy one. It is even possible that happiness and knowledge may be in some ways incompatible, so that we are still to-day faced with the choice, which the Greeks propounded long ago, between a happy pig or an unhappy Socrates. This fact need not, however, cause distress, since the question whether happiness is the only thing which is desirable is itself a philosophical question, capable of being answered in different ways.

In what sense a 'Good'? The result is that when the lecturer on philosophy is faced with the inevitable question, 'What's the good of it?' he is reluctantly compelled to admit that, unlike psycho-analysis, which enables you to diagnose the foibles of your friends, or literature, which provides you with suitable topics for intellectual conversation, or science, which enables you to ride in a motor car, philosophy has no direct value.

And, let us be frank about it, this is a severe criticism. Our age, governed pre-eminently by the stomach and pocket view of life, demands of whatever is proffered for its approval that it shall deliver 'the goods'. Hence non-vocational education, education that is to say which does not confer any specifiable advantage in the struggle for existence, is regarded with disfavour. In the newer Universities of America, for example, the so-called practical subjects, engineering, agriculture, or medicine, are exclusively studied, while pure mathematics, philosophy, and even history are neglected. Something of the same attitude is spreading to the older American Universities, and it would require more hardihood than I, for one, can command to maintain that the same tendency is not perceptible here. After all, we say, we pay for education, and we demand in return that it should pay us.

That this is a just demand I should be the last to deny; but it is important that we should not unduly restrict the notion of what constitutes payment. Bread and butter and a good position in the world are certainly payment. But what of the capacity for clear thinking, the sympathy and tolerance that come from a lively understanding of the views and difficulties of others, and the habit of disinterested intellectual inquiry? Do these not add to the fullness and richness of our lives? The modern world answers on the whole that they do not. And here philosophy steps in to take up the challenge which this answer implies, one of the most important of the incidental effects of philosophy being to call in question the whole scale of values upon which the conventional attitude is based. What, the philosopher will ask, is the point of achieving a good position in life, if you have no conception of right living when you have achieved it? And he may then proceed to point out that right living embraces just those non-material goods which philosophy seeks to realize, in the absence of which even the most materially successful life may be said to have failed. Thus the study of philosophy may cause us to renounce the very standards by which philosophy is condemned. But this is to anticipate.

Absence of Results. I turn to the second count in the indictment, that, unlike science, philosophy presents us with no definite results. If by definite results is meant a complete set of agreed answers to all the questions that have puzzled mankind since speculation began, it must be admitted that philosophy has none to show. The philosopher, instead of building upon the foundations laid by his predecessor, spends much of his energy in criticizing those who have gone before, disputing their hypotheses and throwing doubt on their conclusions. There is no one philosophy to which all philosophers will agree, as there is, for example, one multiplication table to which all mathematicians agree. Many of the disputes of philosophers are, moreover, disputes about what exactly it is that they are disputing about. Hence arises the gibe that a philosopher is like a blind man looking in a dark room for a black cat that isn't there.

Having now frankly stated the charges against philosophy, and pointed out the respects in which they are well grounded, let us see what answer philosophy has to make in her defence. In the first place, the charge that philosophy arrives at no definite conclusions, though true in a sense, is true only in a highly Pickwickian one. All the sciences started life as philosophy. Astronomy, mathematics, biology and physics were branches of philosophy in the time of the Greeks, and, for so long as they were purely speculative in character, philosophy they remained. So soon, however, as anything definite came to be known about them, they seceded from philosophy and became separate sciences in their own right. Philosophy is thus in the unfortunate position of a schoolmaster, who loses his pupils directly they show promise.

Definite knowledge has no place in philosophy, and it is in this aloofness from brute fact that men have found much of its charm. Let us assume for a moment that philosophy is entirely inconclusive, and never does and never can increase the stock of our information about the universe. Is it, therefore, valueless? If we put philosophy at the very lowest valuation, and admit the very worst that has been said of it, it becomes a kind of game. The game is that of discovering the reasons for what we wish to believe upon instinct; yet to find these reasons is none the less an instinct. It is the instinct of intellectual curiosity, and it is an instinct which only philosophy can fully satisfy. It is admitted that the body requires exercise to keep it in condition, and football, boxing, and gymnastics are praised even by utilitarians. But the mind requires exercise just as much as the body, and philosophy, which is the gymnastics of the mind, is the pursuit which above all others spring-cleans the mind and keeps it in training. This is done by argument and dialectic. Argument can be amusing, and there is no argument like a philosophical argument. Its very inconclusiveness is its fascination. Every argument about facts comes to an abrupt termination when the facts are known. If you have an argument with a man about the time at which a train leaves London for Newcastle, there will always come a stage at which someone will fetch the time-table and look it up. When this has happened, there is no more to be said. Thus every argument except a philosophical argument is at the mercy of the man who knows. Now the production of fact stifles the exercise of intelligence by rendering it unnecessary. We only think when we do not know. Philosophy, which is the only form of study which yields no definite results, alone emancipates its followers from the limitations of factual knowledge.

The Widening of the Common-sense World. But philosophy is more than a game, and influences our lives in ways which are more profound than those of mental athletics. This practical influence of philosophy is exerted in a number of different ways. Philosophy will take a common object and show us that we know much less about it than we expected. A chair, for example, which appears to common sense to be four wooden legs surmounted by a square wooden seat, can be shown by philosophical reflection to be an idea in the mind of God, a colony of souls, a collection of sense data, a piece of our own psychology, or a modification of the Absolute. Philosophy can give very good reasons for supposing that the chair is each and all of these things, and, although it cannot definitely prove which of them it is, it at least makes it quite certain that it is not *just* a chair. From this point of view the value of philosophy lies largely in its uncertainty. The man who has no acquaintance with philosophy goes through life imprisoned in the prejudices, the preferences, and the habitual beliefs derived from the society in which he happens to have been born and the period in which he lives. If he is born in Persia, he thinks it right to have four wives; if in England, only one. If he is born in 400 B.C., he thinks the sun goes round the earth; if in A.D. 1900, he takes the contrary view. None of the views which he holds are the result of independent thought; all are the product of convictions which, having grown up without the consent of his reason, are merely the reflections of the conventions and prejudices of his age. To such a one the world tends to become dull and obvious. Common objects provoke no questions, and unfamiliar possibilities are contemptuously rejected. Philosophy, which raises doubts about what has hitherto been taken for granted, keeps alive the sense of wonder and restores mystery to the world. By diminishing our certainty as to what is, it enormously increases the possibility of what may be. Thus it makes life more interesting, not because of the answers it provides to the questions it raises, but because, by the mere process of raising such questions, it liberates us from the dominance of the actual and sets us on the threshold of the region of emancipating thought.

Philosophy as a Clearing House. It is here that we approach the specific function of philosophy, a function which philosophy can alone fufil and which constitutes its main justification. We can exhibit this function in the clearest light by drawing attention to the fundamental difference between philosophy and science. The scientist, working away in a watertight compartment, devotes his attention to a certain section of the universe. Thus enclosed, he arrives at more or less definite conclusions without stopping to think what relation they bear to the conclusions reached by other scientists working in their watertight compartments. This is not a criticism of the scientist; cosmic correlation is not his business, but it is not to be wondered at if some of the conclusions clash. Some of the results of modern physics are, for example, at the moment incompatible with the findings of a well-known school of psychologists, so that, if what certain physicists say about the world is true, what certain psychologists say cannot be true. Hence arises the need of a clearing

I. Philosophy and Life

house in which the results arrived at by the various sciences can be pooled and collated, in order that, looking at them as a whole, we may be able to infer what kind of universe it is that we live in, and hazard a guess at the destiny of human life within it.

Now philosophy may be defined as the effort to comprehend the universe as a whole, not, like physics or biology, a special department of it, but the whole mass of data to which the moral intuitions of the ordinary man, the religious consciousness of the saint, the æsthetic enjoyment of the artist, and the history of the human race, no less than the discoveries of the physicist and the biologist, contribute. To look for certain fixed and definite knowledge in regard to a subject matter of so all-embracing a character is unreasonable.

In the first place, the subject matter is itself in a state of continual flux. It is not philosophy alone that is changing and self-contradictory; the record of science is strewn with the debris of discarded theories, and the scientific laws and formulæ of one age are superseded in the next. At the moment the physicists are presenting us with new theories about the constitution of the material universe at the rate of one every ten years, while biology is in a perpetual state of controversy about the cause and character of the evolution of life. But more important than differences in the data about which the philosopher speculates are the differences in the minds of philosophers. Philosophy is not content to catalogue the facts; it inquires into their meaning. Pooling the experiences of the scientist, the saint, the

artist, and the common man, it asks what must be the
nature of the universe in which such experiences are
possible. It is interested, in other words, not so much
in the facts as in their significance. Thus it establishes
principles of selection and rejection whereby some of
the facts are shown to be important, while others are
rejected as trivial or condemned as illusory; it assigns
values too, and assesses the universe in respect of its
beauty or its goodness.

The Subjective Element. Now, this search for meaning
and significance, this task of assessment and valuation,
involve considerations of a highly personal character.
We shall select according to what we think important;
we shall group and arrange according to likenesses
which we think significant; we shall assign values to
what we recognize as beautiful or good. What we think
important or significant or beautiful or good will depend very largely upon the sort of minds we possess,
and not only upon our minds, but also upon our
characters and temperaments. One man will detect
common elements where another observes only a chaos
of differences; some will recognize the hand of God in
what others insist to be a haphazard collection of
fortuitous events. Thus, while the facts are the same
for all, the conclusions which we base upon them
will be different. Nor need this difference be deplored;
just as it takes all sorts of men to make a world, so
does it take all sorts of minds to make the truth about
the world, and philosophy is no more to be dismissed

I. Philosophy and Life

because each philosopher has a different system, than morality is to be invalidated by the fact of differing moral judgments, or religion proclaimed to be nonsense because there are innumerable variations of religious belief.

The conclusions of philosophy are, therefore, uncertain because they depend not upon facts but upon the interpretation of facts; and, once we go beyond the facts and attempt to give them a meaning, we have to reckon with the element of personality. Given the same facts, two observers will take different views of what they mean, simply because they are different people. The facts upon which men's creeds, for example, are based are the same for all, yet there is no view about the universe, however fantastic, which has not been held by some, and it is possible to find excellent reasons for holding any belief under the sun. It is easy to see, then, that our attitude to facts and our estimate of their significance are in part determined by our temperaments, our experiences, our wishes, and our hopes; so much so, that it often seems as if our reason was given to us only in order that we might invent arguments for what we instinctively wish to believe. Our hopes and our wishes are, no doubt, pretty much the same, however we choose to disguise them, but there are undeniable differences; the heaven for which the Mohammedan craves, a heaven devoted to perpetual love making, seems to me, for example, as intolerable as the old-fashioned Christian's conception of an orgy of laudatory singing. All that I wish to emphasize here, however, is the undeniable part which our wishes play in influencing our conclusions. Once this is admitted, it will be seen that every philosophy is in some sense a personal statement. It is a picture of the universe, it is true, but it is also a reflection of the philosopher.[1] This personal factor must be discounted in assessing the truth-claim of a philosophy. The scientist points to the universe and says: 'This is a fact'; the philosopher can only draw his inferences and say, 'I think this is implied by the fact'. You may agree with him because you are constrained by the cogency of his reasoning; you may also agree merely because you happen to share his wishes.

Universality of Philosophic Themes. Hence the uncertainty of philosophy arises partly from the largeness of the questions it studies, and partly from the temperamental considerations which must necessarily affect our attitude to them. But the all-embracing character of philosophical problems, while it makes for uncertainty in the answers, is not without its effect upon the mind that studies them. Taking the whole realm of knowledge for its sphere, philosophy deals with those ultimate problems which have troubled men in all ages since thought began. For equipment to grapple with these problems philosophy arms itself with the most up-to-date information, including, of course, the conclusions reached by the special sciences. But the philosopher, as we have seen, is not content to rest in these conclusions; they are for him merely a stimulus to speculation, diving-boards from which he may plunge into

[1] But never solely of the philosopher. See Chapter V, p. 167.

the sea of the unknown. His work begins, in short, where that of the scientist leaves off. In the light of the facts recorded by scientific research, he proceeds to a renewed consideration of the time-honoured problems of humanity. Has the universe any plan or purpose, or is it merely a fortuitous concourse of atoms? Is mind a fundamental feature of the universe, in terms of which we are ultimately to interpret the rest, or is it a mere accident, an eddy in the primeval slime, doomed one day to finish its pointless journey with as little significance as it began it? Are good and evil real and ultimate principles existing independently of men, or are they merely the names we give to the things of which we happen to approve and to disapprove?

Philosophy seeks to study these questions impartially, not desiring to arrive at results which are comfortable or flattering to human conceit, nor to construct a universe which is conformable with human wishes. On the contrary, it endeavours to maintain a modest attitude towards objective fact, and to discover truth without fear or favour.

The Philosophic Attitude. Those who give time to the study of such impersonal questions are bound to preserve something of the same impartiality and freedom in the world of action and emotion. Since a consideration of fundamental questions shows us how little is certainly known, the philosopher is ready to grant that contrary views may have as much or as little truth as his own. Thus philosophy generates an attitude of tolerance which refuses to make the distinction between right and wrong, good and evil, truth and falsehood, identical with that between the things done and the views held by the self and the contrary actions and thoughts of others. Finally, the fact that no agreed answer has yet been discovered to the most fundamental questions cannot but suggest to the honest thinker that all systems hitherto constructed are in some degree false. Those who have no tincture of philosophy are inclined on all questions not susceptible of proof to supply the place of knowledge by converting other people's conjectures into dogmas. The philosopher, on the other hand, will admit that even his so-called knowledge is conjectural, and regard fanaticism, bigotry, and dogmatism not only as an offence against manners, but as a betrayal of the truth. It is for the sake of the questions themselves which philosophy studies, and of the methods with which it pursues them, rather than for any set of answers that it propounds, that philosophy is to be valued.

Through the greatness of the universe which it contemplates the mind itself achieves greatness. It escapes from the circle of petty aims and desires which for most of us constitute the prison of everyday life, and forgetting the nervous little clod of wants and ailments which is the self, is elevated into communion with that which is greater than the self. On the practical side this greatness of the mind generates qualities of tolerance, justice and understanding, in the growth of which lies the chief hope for the world to-day.

Chapter VIII

Life into Value

★

I. RELEVANCE TO BOOK OF PHILOSOPHICAL POSITION

I have hinted on a number of occasions in the preceding chapters that a particular position which has been adopted, or a particular line of argument which has been followed can ultimately be justified only on the assumption of some general philosophical position. This is, I take it, as it should be. If one ventures to have such a thing as a philosophy—and the venture, rash enough at all times, becomes increasingly so with every fresh encroachment by science and erosion by psychology—it should, just because it is a philosophy and purports therefore to be an affirmation about the universe as a whole, apply with more or less relevance to every subject of philosophic discourse.

If, in other words, you have come to hold some definite view—however tentatively and however conscious you may be of the difficulties and objections to which it is exposed—on such fundamental questions as the ultimate character of the universe, whether, for example, it is mental or material or neither or both, the status of life in general within the universe, the significance of human life in particular, the nature of the evolutionary process which has produced human life, the purpose, if any, of that process, the status of values and their relation to the knowing mind—you will find it impossible to keep this general view entirely in the background, when you are discussing topics such as the function of reason and the recognition of values in the modern world, with which I have been concerned in the preceding chapters.

I have more especially been conscious of the intrusion of this general view, or, rather, of the pressure it was exerting upon me to permit its intrusion, in the third chapter and in the seventh. In the third chapter, I endeavoured to convey my belief in the objectivity of values and the special significance of the experiences involved in the apprehension of them. In the last, I described what I conceive to be the function and value of philosophy. Yet, although both chapters were of an apologetic rather than a constructive character, being concerned to defend objective value and to vindicate the claims of reasoning against the logical relativism, the scientific empiricism, the psychological subjectivism and the moral and the æsthetic anarchy of the times, I found my defence hampered from the outset by two disabilities. Either I had to assume positions for which I believed I had good warrant, but for which I had produced no grounds, or I had to dispense with the very valuable assistance to my cause which the assumption of just those positions would have enabled me to derive. The dilemma was an uncomfortable one, and struggling first on one and then upon the other of its horns, but principally upon the first, I endeavoured to console myself and appease my reader by promising in a later chapter some indication of the general framework of philosophical assumptions within which the positions I was wishing to assume would naturally fall, and from which they would logically derive.

Difficulty of Summarizing a Philosophy. Yet now that the time has come to carry out this implied promise, I am dismayed by the difficulty of fulfilling the obligation it imposes. I have endeavoured to set out elsewhere, in books entitled *Matter, Life and Value*[1], and *Philosophical Aspects of Modern Science*[2], the reasons for the positions which I have hitherto assumed and now seek to support. Both books are long, the first one formidably so; hence the task that now devolves upon me is summarily to recast the arguments there detailed at length. This at least would have been my task, were it not that my views have undergone some inevitable changes since these books were written, and a mere summary will not, therefore, fill the bill.

Even if it did, I find on consideration that I cannot bring myself to undertake it. Not only is the task of summarizing a dull one, but I am certain that I should botch it. Now diffident as I may be about the conclusions I have reached, and inadequate as I suspect many of the arguments I have used in their favour to be, I have

[1] Oxford University Press. 1929.
[2] Allen and Unwin. 1932.

sufficient interest in the conclusions, sufficient respect for the arguments not to wish to do them the injustice of misstating them. Consequently I must content myself with running over the main heads of my philosophical credo, in so far as they are relevant to the issues raised in this book, leaving those who care to know the reasons for them to look elsewhere.

II. STATEMENT OF BELIEF
A. KNOWLEDGE AND ITS OBJECTS

Reversion to the Concept of Mental Levels. In the third chapter I referred to the account given in Plato's *Symposium* of the way in which the Form of Beauty comes to be apprehended by the human mind. The distinguishing characteristic of the process was, it may be remembered, the series of 'jumps' by means of which the development of æsthetic insight was effected. The advance from one level of apprehension to another was discontinuous, and the final revelation of the Form, described in the language of a mystical vision, appeared to be divorced from the logical process which had led up to and conditioned it. I laid some stress in the chapter in question upon this conception of discontinuous advance, this 'jumping' by the mind, and considered its bearing upon the appreciation of art. I now affirm my belief that it is equally fruitful in metaphysics, that it is in truth only a particular illustration of a general process, the process whereby the mind comes to know the universe outside it.

Life into Value

The external world is, I hold, revealed to the human mind precisely as it is. I use the word 'revealed' deliberately, to indicate that we in no sense create or even contribute to what we know. The process of knowing is, I hold, one of discovering what is there, not of imputing or creating what is not. Such discovery takes place just as truly when we are thinking about the relations which hold between so-called abstract conceptions, as when we are perceiving that the fire is hot, the circle round and the sky blue. The world so revealed appears to be arranged in a series of orders or levels. I do not mean that the levels differ in degrees of reality, as many philosophers have supposed. In fact I am unable to see how any one thing can be more *real* than another. They differ, so far as concerns our present purpose, primarily in respect of the order in which they come to be known by the developing mind.

We often make use meaningfully of the expression, 'the mind develops'. Yet the statement is an ambiguous one which is capable of diverse interpretations. I suggest that the one which it can most suitably bear is that of a sharpening and widening of the mind's faculty of knowledge or awareness, so that, as a consequence of its development, more of the world outside us is revealed to the knowing mind, than was revealed before. If this is so, the degree of development of any mind may be measured by reference to the area of the universe revealed to it. A highly developed mind is one aware not only of more of the contents of the world, but of different kinds of contents and, in particular, of contents more difficult of discernment than those accessible to a mind less developed, just as the ears of dogs and savages can discern notes whose pitch renders them inaudible to civilized human beings.

Knowledge of Sense Data. The order of contents immediately revealed to the minds of animals and babies consists of what philosophers are accustomed to call sense data. These are not physical objects, but the patches of colour of which we are actually aware when we see something, the sounds which we apprehend when we hear something, the smells which we smell when we smell it, and so forth. Sugar, we say, is white; it is also sweet. But when we put it into our mouths, the sweetness we taste is not white, nor, when we look at it, is the white patch we see sweet. When we look at a table we do not see the whole of it; we see a brown shape which varies in appearance as we alter our point of observation. When we rap it, we hear a short, sharp noise; when we feel it, we are aware of a hard, cool something. Now the theory of sense data asserts that these data of sense, the brown shape, the sharp noise, the hard, cool something, constitute the actual contents of the outside world of which our senses make us immediately aware. It is through them, by virtue of some process of integration and synthesis, that we somehow come to know sugar and tables; but this knowledge which we presently come to have of sugar and tables is not sensory knowledge.

Life into Value

Knowledge of Physical Objects. By saying that it is not sensory, I mean, among other things, that it is not knowledge which we possess as babies. The process whereby the fragmentary data of sense become synthesized into objects by the infant mind is studied by psychologists. Thus the something which feels soft to its touch, the something which is pink to look at and the pleasantly cooing something, which are the baby's primitive sensations of the object which it subsequently comes to know as its mother, gradually become integrated, by virtue of the fact that they are always found to go together, into a physical object, a human body, which is both soft and pink and the source of a cooing noise.

The relation of sense data to physical objects is obscure, and I cannot go into it here. There seems, however, to be good reason for thinking that sense data are neither parts of the surfaces of physical objects nor caused by them. All we can say with any degree of certainty is that the mind first knows fragmentary sense data, and then synthesizes these fragmentary data into physical objects. But the knowledge of the physical object which is thus attained is not itself sensory knowledge; it is the result of a definite jump by the mind from one level of apprehension to another, a jump which only minds at a certain level of development are capable of making. It would surprise me very much to find that a mollusc's world contained physical objects which were in the least like our 'objects'. But I should not be surprised, if a mollusc writing the story of his life experiences, were found to be talking in terms of felt, smelt and tasted substances,[1] analogous to the shape we feel in the dark and wonder *what* it is, to the unpleasant odour that assails our nostrils prompting us to ask '*What* made that smell?', and the bitter flavour which we experience in the salad when, munching lettuce, we subsequently discover that we have bitten on a caterpillar. And when, having asked ourselves the question, '*What* is it that we are feeling, smelling, tasting,' we answer it is a table, a dead mouse, or a caterpillar, there is, I suggest, a definite jump on the part of the mind to a new level of awareness, the jump from sense data to physical objects.

Knowledge of Objects of Thought. But the mind of civilized man does not remain at the level of the awareness of physical objects; it proceeds to the apprehension of objects of thought. And just as practice and exercise in the knowledge of sense data prepared the way for the mind's jump to the knowledge of physical objects, so practice and exercise in the knowledge of physical objects lead to the apprehension of the relations between them, relations which, since they are not themselves regarded as 'physical' even by courtesy title, I am terming 'objects of thought'. They lead, for instance, to an apprehension of the causal relation.

This is not the place for a discussion of the vexed

[1] I do not wish to commit myself to the doubtful proposition that molluscs have noses and palates. This is a hypothetical illustration merely; it is not intended as natural history.

philosophical problem of 'cause'. I must content myself, therefore, with a statement of philosophical belief
without giving the highly controversial grounds for it.
I believe that what happens when we apprehend the
fact that A *causes* B is more or less as follows: We see
a stone travel through the air and hit the window of a
house. Immediately afterwards we see a hole in the
window and fragments of glass falling to the ground. We
say that the stone broke the window and made the hole;
we affirm, in fact, a causal relation between the stone
and the hole, but we do not apprehend the relation
with our senses, we do not *see* it as we *see*, or think we
see, the stone and the hole. So far as *sense perception* is
concerned, all that we are aware of is first, the succession
of sensory data which we call 'a moving stone', secondly,
the sensory data which we call 'a hole in window'. It
is, nevertheless, a fact that we *are* aware of the causal
relation. I *know* that the moving stone was the cause of
the smashed window, just as surely as I know the stone
and the window. If anybody says that I don't know it,
merely because I do not apprehend it with my senses,
he is saying what is not true.

What account, then, are we to give of this knowledge?
I would suggest—and, I repeat, I am only stating a
view, not defending it—that there are certain characteristics of reality, certain facts which belong to the nature
of things, certain constituents of the universe—the
precise language used here is immaterial—which, while
not revealed either to sense perception or to introspec-
tion, are nevertheless known. And they are known by

means of a faculty which only minds at a certain level of development have evolved, a faculty which may be called 'Non-Perceptual Intuition'. All relations between physical things are, I should say, of this type; so are ethical characteristics; so are categories such as those of quantity, quality, substance and physical force. They are, that is to say, objects of thought.

Objects of thought are incapable of manifesting themselves sensuously as do colours, sounds and smells, yet it is necessary that we should have sensory experience to draw our attention to their presence in the universe. Just as experience of sense data sooner or later directs the attention of the mind which has the experience to the physical objects to which the data point, so experience of physical objects sooner or later directs the attention of the mind which has the experience to the non-perceptual relations and categories which relate the perceived objects. But, as in the former case, so in this one, it is necessary that the minds having the experience should have reached a certain level of development, in order that they may be in a position to make the jump involved from the apprehension of one type of object to the apprehension of another. And, that the mind may reach this level, exercise and practice at the preceding level of habitual apprehension are necessary. It was, in other words, only by long reflection upon phenomena such as the breaking of the window by the stone, that men's minds came to grasp the general concept of cause.

Life into Value

Analysis of Thinking. In my view the process which we call thinking, the process which is now habitual in the human race, is nothing more or less than the exploration by the faculty of Non-Perceptual Intuition of regions of the universe which are not accessible to the senses, and of the relations between the objects in those regions. Just as in sense perception the mind acquaints itself with the physical contents of the world, reporting on the smells, tastes, shapes, colours, sounds and so forth which it contains, so, in thinking, it becomes acquainted with contents of a different order revealed not to the senses but directly to the faculty of Non-Perceptual Intuition.

It is, of course, the case that many philosophers are inclined to doubt whether in thinking the mind is aware of anything but its own ideas. But, if this were so, it is difficult to see in what sense it could be maintained that some of our ideas are true and some false. True ideas are, presumably, those which correspond with or faithfully represent some aspect of or factor in reality. If, then, we do not merely have ideas but can know, as we undoubtedly do know in the case of some of them, that they are true, it would seem that we must also credit ourselves with the ability to know the aspects of or factors in reality with which our ideas correspond or which they faithfully represent, in order that, noting the correspondence, we may proceed to affirm of the ideas that they are true. Moreover, it is hard to see how the fact that one man's thought can be communicated to or made intelligible to another is to be accounted for, if they are never thinking of the same thing; yet it is precisely this that, on the assumption that each in thinking is aware only of *his own private ideas*, they never can do.

Thinking of Cæsar. Consider, for example, the case of historical thinking. Let us suppose that I am thinking of the fact that Cæsar crossed the Rubicon. Of what am I aware when I think of Cæsar? Certainly not of a physical object, since Cæsar, as a physical object, has ceased to exist, or rather, the substance of his physical body is by now so diffused through worms, soil, grass, cattle and other people, that it would be exceedingly difficult for me to think of such a thing, even if I wanted to. But in fact it is quite certain that it is not of any such diffusion of physical substances that I am thinking, when I reflect upon the fact that Cæsar crossed the Rubicon. Is Cæsar, then, an idea or concept in my own mind, and is it of this idea or concept that I am thinking, when I affirm that Cæsar crossed the Rubicon?

There seem to me to be two conclusive reasons against this view. First, there is the difficulty already cited, namely that, if it were true, the mind of each historian would be entirely occupied with his own ideas and no two historians could ever think of the same thing. If historians never think of the same thing, one does not see how they could fruitfully discuss historical matters, or even intelligibly communicate the results of their reflections. Now it does seem to be the case that historians do sometimes intelligibly communicate. Secondly, if historical objects, such as Cæsar or the battle of Waterloo, are ideas and only ideas in the minds of those who think about them, the abolition of minds would involve the abolition of historical objects. This means that, should there come a time when all knowledge of history ceases, either as the result of the destruction of the human race or of the diversion of its mental activity to some possibly more profitable pursuit, historical facts would cease to exist, and it would cease to be a fact that the battle of Waterloo was fought in 1815. Now I can see no more reason for supposing that this would be the case, than I can for supposing that my table would cease to be square, if I ceased to look at it.

I conclude, then, that historical objects are not ideas in my mind but are public objects, of the kind which I have called objects of thought, that they are independent of all minds, and that, in common with all non-perceptual objects, they are directly apprehended by minds which have reached a certain level of development.

III. STATEMENT OF BELIEF
B. ART AS THE WINDOW OF REALITY

Intimations of a New Level of Apprehension. At the level at which the minds of civilized human beings normally function to-day, objects of thought and the relations between them mainly occupy their attention. But we have, I believe, reached a stage of evolution at which there is being gradually evolved the capacity for the apprehension of another order of objects, which I propose to call 'objects of value'. This capacity appears at present intermittently and uncertainly and appears mainly in mystics and artists.

At every stage of evolution there are 'sports', precocious children of the species, who are in advance of their contemporaries, pointing forward to what the species may become, rather than typically representing it as it is. It is precisely this precocity which distinguishes the artist and the mystic. For in what respect do they differ from the rest of us? Primarily in respect of their vision, a vision which is at once more subtle and more penetrating. Common phraseology is near the mark when it speaks of the artist as one who is able to *see* more in a given situation than his fellows. The 'more' which he sees is the significant form which lies hid in common objects; he discerns, that is to say, within the material medium which overlays and obscures them, certain combinations of forms which, I suggest, derive their significance from the fact that by some means or other they introduce us to this new class of objects, which I am proposing to call 'objects of value'. To revert to common language, the artist detects the manifestation of beauty in what the ordinary man sees only as an object of everyday use. So long as his vision lasts, the artist remains rapt in contemplation, thrilled to ecstasy by the image of this new order of being which is vouchsafed to him. But the vision does not last. Life is a dynamic, changing force, an ever restless surge, which, though it may ultimately come to rest in the untrammelled contemplation of objects of value, has not yet emerged at a stage at which such contemplation is either possible or desirable. The most that has yet been vouchsafed even to its favoured children is a fleeting and intermittent glimpse. The veil is lifted only to be redrawn. While æsthetic contemplation lasts, we are willless and selfless, but only for the moment. Scarcely is he assured of the unique character of what his vision reveals, before the artist is caught up again into the stream of life, and pulled back into the world of need and want, of struggle and desire, which is the habitual type of human experience at our present level.

Why the Artist Creates. And filled with longing and regret for the vision that was his, but is his no longer, he strives to embody its outlines on canvas or in stone before the memory of it shall have utterly passed away. Thus the work of art is a witness not so much to the artist's vision as to his failure to retain it. It is because he cannot hold his awareness of the real, that he makes images and copies in which his remembrance of it is embodied. In these images and copies the sensuous material, with which significant form is in natural objects overlaid, is so reduced, that the combinations whose significance the artist has caught are thrown up into relief, being presented as clearly as the nature of the material medium allows. For this reason, because the artist has first prepared the way, it is easier for those of us who are not gifted with his powers of vision to see beauty in works of art than it is in natural objects.

The Inevitability of Great Art

The Inevitability of Great Art. The ability to reveal to us something which we could never have discovered for ourselves, but whose rightness, whose inevitability even, when perceived is at once recognized, is one of the distinguishing characteristics of great art. How often in listening for the first time to a Mozart quartet has the development of a movement seemed to me, in the light of what has preceded, to be inevitable. So surely do I anticipate, that I hear, almost as it were in advance, the bars which my mind has foreshadowed. The movement proceeds and, surprisingly, what follows is completely different from anything I had imagined; different and infinitely better. For a moment I am startled, even shocked. 'How', I wonder, 'could Mozart have committed himself to such abrupt, such startling transitions, which consort so ill with what has gone before?' The feeling of surprise passes, to be followed by a sudden delighted recognition that the music was, after all, completely right. Though I could never have imagined them for myself, the surprising phrases, once their import is grasped, are seen to be the only possible development of the theme. My foreshadowed continuation, I now realize, was utterly banal and commonplace.

In much the same way when I am reading the great novelists, a person will seem to me to say or to do something which is completely out of character. I get this feeling more particularly with Dickens. Little Dorrit, for example, 'the prison flower', makes a remark about her father which shows her unexpectedly and, to the reader quite shockingly, to have been contaminated by her prison environment. The feeling of inappropriateness lasts, but only for a moment; then the apparent departure from character is seen to be in fact 'in character'. Herein, to quote Sir Arthur Quiller-Couch, is 'the true novelist's stroke; rightly divined, so suddenly noted that we, who had not expected it, consent at once with a "Yes, yes—of course, it happened so".'

The Function of Great Art. Plato was inclined to interpret the somewhat similar feeling, a feeling which expresses itself in the words 'But, of course, I see it now. I really knew it all the time, only I did not realize that I knew it', which we experience when we suddenly *see* the solution of a mathematical problem, or suddenly grasp the significance of an initially puzzling logical demonstration, as evidence for the doctrine of pre-existence. The feeling of familiarity with which the solution or the demonstration eventually comes home to us, is, he thinks, evidence of our having somehow known it before and forgotten what we knew. I concede the feeling of familiarity. I would go further than Plato and postulate it for those unexpected turns of phrase in music or of character in fiction, which first surprise then reassure us with their artistic inevitability, their complete rightness. But I venture here to suggest as an alternative explanation the sudden opening of the eye of the layman's soul by the vision of the artist to a glimpse of the world of value. It is a world to which we could not have penetrated by ourselves; but, once viewed, it evokes the feelings of rightness, of appropriateness, of inevitability to which I have referred. Thus, art is the window through which life gets its first intimation of the nature of a new order of objects which belong to the world of value; its function is, to use a metaphor of Plato's, to turn the eye of the soul round to reality, by revealing the element of significant form in virtue of which the objects of the material world show forth the patterns of the world of value which lie behind them. Yet it is not Beauty itself that the artist contemplates, but only the image of Beauty in a material setting; it is only the mystic who may contemplate Beauty and Truth directly, and he, for reasons into which I cannot fully enter here, is not allowed to indulge his vision overmuch.

For the world of value is a shining glory, the direct vision of which man is unable to endure. Yet the glory shines through the veil of sense and the alert and receptive mind catches its reflection in common things. The artist and the musician are seekers after that glory, and the haunting beauty that they pursue is the reflection of its light. At times they may even catch a glimpse of the original itself, and, seeing it, are transported with delight. But their vision, if indeed they have it, is never more than a fleeting glimpse. For a continuous vision the soul of man is not as yet prepared. Faced with a direct view of reality, it falters and falls back, and, were not the veil of matter mercifully interposed, it would be stunned and blinded by the force and glory of reality; thus it must content itself with the images which we call works of art.

Life into Value

Two points remain to complete this preliminary sketch. First, just as in the earlier stages of mind's development, practice and experience at each level of apprehension that was successively reached prepared the way for the mind's jump to a higher level, so it is by long and loving familiarity with objects of thought that the mind is prepared for its jump to the apprehension of objects of value. It is the scholar rather than the peasant or the halfwit who is likely to respond to art and to see the beauty in the world.

Logic Transcended. Of the nature of this jump, in so far as it is made by the artist creating or the critic appreciating beauty, I have already written in the third chapter, and, as this is not a treatise on æsthetics, I have little to add here. One thing only, and this is my second point, I would stress. Once the jump from one level of mental awareness to another has been made, the rules and canons of criticism appropriate to the preceding level cease to apply.

Thus it is a sign that the jump to the level of value has been made, when logic is replaced by insight. The vision of the Form of Beauty which Plato describes in the *Symposium* has no affinity with the intellectual process, the process of exact thinking in science and mathematics, which leads up to it. Ordinarily we expect people who have enjoyed some peculiarly delightful or exciting experience to be able to report it, or, at least, to give some account of it. But nobody expects from the mystic a coherent account, still less a logical explanation of the vision that has transported him. Similarly with art. The greatest art seems to be independent of the rules of composition which determine excellence at a lower level. In fact, the greatest writers may and habitually do break all the rules without prejudicing their claim to greatness.

The Art which is beyond Criticism. Everybody can point to obvious faults in great works of literature. In *The Merry Wives*, for example, or in *King Lear*, there are faults of composition and faults of form; there is incoherence; there are improbabilities and inconsistencies. We could no doubt improve the plots of both plays considerably. Yet both reach a certain level, a level of what for want of a better word we call 'greatness', at which such criticisms, relevant to smaller works, seem to be negligible. In fact the best *negative* indication of greatness in a work of literary art that I can think of is its indifference, its superiority to mistakes which would wreck a production at the ordinary level. A work is great, when it has ceased to matter that it is bad. More formally we may define greatness as a characteristic of works of art, which they possess in virtue of the vision they embody of an order of the universe which transcends the objects of thought upon which the minds of most civilized men are normally directed. This order is that which contains objects of value. Thus the apprehension of the great artist is an apprehension of value.

I have spoken so far of literary greatness; but greatness in literature illustrates a quality which to my mind is more completely and more convincingly exemplified by music. There are certain passages in music which, even when they observe, seem to transcend all the ordinary rules of composition, for example, the slow movement of Bach's D Minor Concerto for two violins and orchestra. There are others equally transcendent which appear to violate them. Sometimes there is in the same movement a transition from music which acknowledges form and keeps the rules, to passages which are apparently void of form and indifferent to rules. This transition is usually gradual; one is insensibly transported to a realm in which excellences of harmony and counterpoint are no longer present, or no longer missed, if they are absent; if they are present, their presence has become irrelevant. Sometimes this happens abruptly. Consider, for instance, the slow movement of Beethoven's Trio in B Flat, Opus 97, a trio which was composed on the threshold of that third period of Beethoven development when he appears to shed the trappings of an art he has transcended, and communes with Beauty direct. The slow movement consists of a theme beautiful, passionate and instinct with longing, which is subsequently developed in a series of variations. At the close the theme is repeated; at least, it is restated, but the restatement never ends. As the end is approached, an arresting chord is struck, there is a half-close, and then the music suddenly goes off into a new world, a formless void of pure sound for which the word 'mystical' seems the only appropriate description. The music is intensely moving; it is music of the highest order; yet its excellence is not that of ordinary music. It is exactly as if Beethoven had broken through from one world into another, as a man may break through a thicket of jungle to come suddenly upon a view of the hills beyond: or as if, having ascended to a new level, a level at which a new order of reality is apprehended, he contemptuously knocks away the scaffolding of form, harmony and counterpoint, by means of which the ascent was made.

The 'Last Periods' of Great Artists. It is noticeable that these passages, to which the world gives the name of 'mystical', occur for the most part in the works of men who have grown old. The Beethoven of the posthumous quartets, the Shakespeare of the *Tempest*, the Plato of the *Timæus*, and I should like to add—for Shaw too, I submit, is a great artist—the Shaw of the first and last plays of *Back to Methuselah*, are men who, having passed beyond the level of awareness and insight at which most artists have drawn their inspiration, have sought to bring back to mankind a report of what they have experienced. A common interpretation of these passages ascribes their peculiar quality to a kind of foreknowledge, a foreknowledge derived from intimations of the world beyond death, vouchsafed to those who are already nearing their end, as a man may ascend a high mountain for a view of the country which he is soon to traverse. Their qualities of serenity and aloofness, their remoteness from the interests of this world, their palpable lack of concern with the emotions that excite, the affairs that intrigue its inhabitants, are ascribed to the circumstance of their authors being already in spirit members of another. For my part, I would suggest rather that the distinctive qualities of the work of great artists grown old are due to their more constant communing with the world of value. Through long years of endeavour and practice of their art on the level at which reflections of Beauty are seen in sensible things, their minds have been prepared for the jump to the higher level, where the veil of sense is broken and Beauty, and it may be Truth—if Truth be wisdom—are viewed direct.

This aloofness, then, that characterizes the 'last period' work of great artists is not that of the soul already in spirit participating in an advance vision of that which in due temporal course it will more fully enjoy: it is rather the aloofness of the mathematician concerned with the relations between the objects of a timeless world. It is precisely this world which at the next level of evolutionary development may, I would suggest, become the concern of most human minds. What significance should be attached to the phrase 'next level of evolutionary development'? The question is one which must be answered, before I can at last return to the defence of philosophy.

IV. STATEMENT OF BELIEF
C. THE EVOLUTIONARY PROCESS

Dualism: Mind and Matter as Independent Reals. Evolu-

tion is, I believe, a real process in time. It is also a purposive process in which life, initially a blind unconscious thrust, seeks to develop an ever higher degree of
consciousness. Height of consciousness is, I have suggested,[1] to be measured by reference to the character of
the objects of which, at different stages of life's development, consciousness achieves awareness. Life, then, is a
real and independent principle, distinct from, although
animating, matter. Since it affirms the separate existence of matter, this doctrine is not in any sense an
idealist one; nor is it materialist, since it also affirms that
life is other than matter and cannot be analysed in
terms of it. My belief, in fact, involves the unfashionable
doctrine of Dualism. How, it may be asked, can Dualism at this time of day be defended? I can only reply:
'Consider the facts.'

Life's Relation to Matter. Life appears in a world of
matter and is initially characterized by a twofold relationship to matter. It knows or is aware of matter and
it is dependent upon it. By life's knowledge of matter, I
mean merely the perception which we as living organisms have of our bodies and of the external world
through our five senses. The perception of their bodies
and of events occurring in their bodies is characteristic
of all living organisms, however lowly their status. Even
plants may be supposed to be aware of their own physical needs. The feeling of physical need, of the need of
hunger for example, or the need for reproduction,

[1] See above, p. 220.

can be shown to be due to bodily changes taking place within the organism; it can be analysed, that is to say, into awareness of events in the material structure of which the body of the organism is composed. Thus a feeling of pain, such as, for example, toothache, may be described as our awareness of certain material occurrences in our bodies. Animals, as compared with plants, are aware not only of their own bodily needs, but also of the world of matter external to their bodies; they are aware, for example, of other animals.[1] But, though the perception of animals extends over a wider range than that of plants, their attention is still directed almost entirely upon sense data, that is upon matter. I say 'almost entirely' because there are traces of rudimentary thinking in animals: it is probable, for example, that they remember, and the analysis of memory can be shown to require the introduction of objects of thought, since it frequently happens, as I have tried to show,[2] that what we think of, when we remember something, no longer exists as a piece of matter. But in animals the knowledge of objects of thought, even if it exists, is precarious and intermittent, and, like the knowledge of value in human beings, must be reckoned a comparatively abnormal occurrence.

Growing Power of Mind over Matter. Savages think a little more than animals, but not much. When, how-

[1] This, of course, is also true in some degree of some plants: there is no sharp dividing line.
[2] See above, p. 227.

ever, we come to civilized man we find a noticeable change, a change which can best be expressed by saying that the centre of interest and attention has shifted from pieces of matter to objects of thought. In order that we may realize how this change has become possible, let us consider the other characteristic of life's twofold relationship to matter, namely, its dependence upon matter.

It is notorious that one of the great achievements of civilization consists in man's mastery over the forces of nature, in other words, in his power over matter. By the construction of appropriate machines we have made not only gravitation our slave, but also electricity and magnetism, atomic attraction, repulsion, polarization, and so forth. We can utilize these forces to transcend our limitations by making for ourselves new limbs outside ourselves to supplement our original bodily inheritance, cranes and elevators to do the work of arms, trains and motors to take the place of legs. We have learned to fly and supply ourselves with wings in the shape of aeroplanes.

Mastery over the Body. In the second place, we attain to an increasing mastery over the matter which constitutes our own bodies. We have changed and continue to change the structure of our bodies by the use to which we put them. Within the comparatively brief period studied by anatomy we have learned to dispense with tails, and we are progressively eliminating organs such as the appendix and growths such as the toenails, for which we have no further use. The urge to think has caused us to achieve an unprecedented growth in brain structure, and the increasing size of the human head adds to the difficulties and dangers of childbirth. These changes have been wrought unconsciously; but we also possess power over the body which we exercise consciously. With each generation that passes, we can prevent the body from decaying for longer periods, and, when at last decay sets in, we can hold life in the body and so prevent dissolution for longer periods. The regeneration of aged bodies is already among the possible developments of medical science. We can turn *crétins* into normal human beings by suitable injections, and are within measurable distance of controlling man's emotional life by regulating the secretions of the ductless glands. Apart altogether from the prospects of determining the sex of our children, we should be able by gland manipulation within the next hundred years to make ourselves choleric or timid, strongly or weaked sexed, at will. Everything points to the view that our present power over the body will be still further increased in the future.

Diminution of Intercourse with Matter. Thus our power has grown both over matter in general and over the matter of which our bodies are composed in particular. Each increase in power over matter diminishes our need to know it. For example, we do less with our hands than our ancestors; we do not carry weights about, defend ourselves from attack, or develop great muscular

strength. We have in fact delegated our intercourse
with material objects to machines, and our intercourse
with machines may be reduced in theory to the necessity for pressing an occasional button. Each fresh advance in applied science, each addition to man's
power over nature that it brings, is, indeed, rightly
interpreted, merely an opportunity for diminishing our
need to know and have intercourse with matter. This
fact is partially obscured by our childish habit of regarding machines as ends in themselves, rather than as
means to ends beyond themselves. Until we have out-
grown this habit, we shall continue to make the mistake
of looking to mechanisms for our interest and of
depending upon them for our pleasure, instead of regarding them merely as energy economizers, whose
raison d'être consists in their ability to release us from the
need to concern ourselves with matter, and so to set us
free to attend to other things. But this mistake, while it
may delay, cannot permanently obstruct the main
development of life away from matter. Meanwhile the
general tendency of the last two thousand years, the
tendency to utilize the extra limbs we have made outside ourselves to carry on our business with matter for
us, is sufficiently obvious. As a result, our knowledge or
awareness of matter is continually diminishing. Compared with the savage whose main activities consist in
using his hands for hunting and fighting, we make but
little use of material, physical objects. So true is this that
the ordinary clerk or professional man can, broadly
speaking, go through the day without using his hands

at all, except to dress and to feed himself and to write, and the lessening intercourse between the hands and matter could be paralleled from the uses of the other limbs. Meanwhile our senses decay as the need for awareness of physical objects grows less; the savage can hear noises to which we are deaf, and our sense of smell grows duller with each generation.

Purpose of Evolutionary Process. The suggestion that I want to make is that evolution is not a blind, haphazard process, as the materialists suppose, but that it is purposive. Putting it crudely we may say that the purpose of life is so to evolve, that life's past and present knowledge of the world of matter and present knowledge of the world of objects of thought may be superseded by a knowledge of the world of value. Initially life is completely dependent upon matter, while matter exclusively occupies its attention. Already, however, as we have seen, life has achieved a certain degree of emancipation as a result of which it has partially freed itself from the necessity to concern itself with matter, and the attention thus liberated is increasingly directed upon objects of thought. Thinking, in other words, is beginning to supersede doing. As thinking becomes habitual, there begins to emerge for the first time the capacity for new kinds of experience to which we give the names of religious, ethical, and æsthetic. These experiences may be interpreted as the mind's knowledge or awareness of a new type of object, which I have called objects of value, of which we are now beginning to have our first uncertain intimations. And just as the experience of objects of thought, which with animals is rare and inter-mittent, has with us become normal, so may thinking come in its turn to be superseded by the continuous experience on the part of life, in its next stage of develop-ment, of objects which belong to the world of value. Thus our future progress may be conceived as one in which, passing beyond thought, we shall reach the level of illumination which the mystic and the artist now enjoy uncertainly and intermittently.

Chapter IX

Defence of Philosophy—II. Philosophy and Value

★

The Grandeur of Philosophic Writing. I come at last to the defence of philosophy. And the defence is, briefly, that, while the objects with which philosophy deals belong primarily to the world of thought, they are situated, if the metaphor may be pardoned, on the furthest confines of that world, so that the mind, which is continuously concerned with them, is liable sooner or later to break through into the world of value. It is in this sense that philosophy is, in a quite literal interpretation of the word, one of the most 'elevating' pursuits of the human mind. It 'elevates' the mind to a stage or level at which it is liable to pass beyond thought and obtain a vision of value.

Plato named certain sciences as 'propædeutic', that is, as leading up to the study of reality. They were those that trained the mind in precision, especially the sciences of measuring, weighing and counting. To the relation between mathematics and philosophy I shall return in a moment. For the present my object is to affirm the view that philosophy is the most pre-eminent of the propædeutic studies of the mind. Without actually introducing the mind to the world of value, it keeps it perpetually occupied on its threshold. It is the proximity of the philosopher's realm, the realm of abstract thought which is his natural province, to the world of value, that is responsible for the exalting quality, a quality as of high literature, which distinguishes the writings of some of the philosophers and makes philosophy so exciting to read. It is as if the barrier that separates us from the world of value were an envelope, an envelope which in certain regions was torn or frayed, so that the glory which is beyond shines through, as the sun will irradiate a thinning veil of mist. Thus it is that those whose minds perpetually dwell in these regions reproduce in their writings something of the brightness, albeit a reflected brightness, with which the world of their habitual preoccupation is pervaded.

It is along these lines that we must, I would suggest, look for an explanation of the generally conceded claim, that philosophical writings may on occasion be appropriately judged by the canons applicable to great literature. The grounds for this claim constitute in large measure my defence of philosophy and I shall consider them in some little detail.

(1) *Nature of Philosophical Objects and Philosophical Knowledge.* The objects with which philosophy is concerned belong scarcely at all to the physical world. It is true that the philosophical theory of perception examines the nature of the objects known by the mind

II. Philosophy and Value

in sensory experience, and considers whether they are
sense data, physical objects, or mental constructions.
It is also true that the most widely held view at the
moment undoubtedly assigns to them a physical status.
But with this exception, the sphere of philosophical enquiry is the sphere not of sense but of thought, and the
objects to which the philosopher's mind is directed
belong entirely to the world of thought. There is an old
controversy in philosophy as to the existence and nature
of what is known as *a priori* knowledge, that is, of knowledge other than the knowledge which we have obtained
through sense experience. The view, which seems to be
almost certainly true,[1] is that we have such knowledge,
but that sense experience is necessary to direct our attention to the fact that we do have it. It is, nevertheless,
independent of sense experience, and it would not
seem, therefore, to be knowledge about the sensory world.
Yet knowledge must have an object, and the appropriate objects of *a priori* knowledge would appear to be
the objects of thought described in the last chapter.

Now philosophical knowledge, like mathematical,
seems to me to be almost entirely of this *a priori* type.
I noticed above[2] that it is characteristic of mathematics
that none of its assertions are about anything in particular, and that we do not know or care whether any of
them are true. As Bertrand Russell puts it, 'mathematics may be defined as the subject in which we never
know what we are talking about, nor whether what we

[1] See Chapter IV, pages 121, 122, for the reasons for this view.
[2] See Chapter V, pages 161, 162.

are saying is true'. The reason is that pure mathematics is concerned with hypotheses and inferences. 'If', mathematics says, 'so and so is the case, then we may infer that something else will be the case.' But it never positively asserts 'so and so is the case'. It makes in fact no positive assertion about the nature of the physical world, nor is it necessary that there should be a physical in order that the conclusions of mathematics should be true.

Philosophy like Mathematics Indifferent to Facts. Philosophy is in similar case. When philosophers discuss 'cause' or 'substance' or the nature of 'judgment', it is a matter completely indifferent to them whether A causes B or is caused by it, what particular kind of substance S has, or precisely what particular judgments P passes; indeed, it would not make the slightest difference to philosophy, if the A's, the B's, the S's and the P's and all particular things, thoughts and persons ceased to exist,[1] although it would undoubtedly make a considerable difference to philosophers. It is this characteristic, which philosophy shares with mathematics, of being concerned not with particular things, but with general truths, not with instances but with laws, that I have in mind when I say that the objects of philosophical enquiry are not physical things but are objects of thought. And it is not, I submit, too fanciful to suggest that, unlike the objects of scientific enquiry which, although

[1] This generalization must be qualified by the exclusion of that part of philosophy which deals with sense perception.

they are not in fact physical test-tubes, chemicals, gases and fluids, but are rather the laws governing the behaviour of these things, do nevertheless continually refer the scientist back to physical things to illustrate and verify the workings of the laws he postulates, the objects of philosophy lie on those confines of the world of thought which are furthest from the physical realm and also .nearest to the realm of value. It is to this fact, I suggest, that the so-called abstractness of philosophy and the traditional aloofness of philosophers from mundane interests are due. The philosopher misses his train, loses his way, does absent-minded things with his belongings, because his mind, normally directed upon the objects of a non-physical world, cannot easily bring its attention to bear upon the contents of the physical one, as a man used to wearing spectacles sees everything blurred and out of focus when he takes them off.

Music in Relation to Matter. I hope that I shall not be thought indefensibly dogmatic,[1] if I assert without qualification that music is the greatest of the arts, or fanciful, if I suggest that its acknowledged superiority may be due to a similar cause. Music, to put the point crudely, makes far less use of matter than any of the other arts. The sculptor manipulates plaster and clay, and his work when finished is marble, bronze or stone. The painter takes as his models material things, and

[1] Partly because I have written at length in Chapter VI of *Matter, Life and Value*, and Chapters IV and IX of *Under the Fifth Rib* in defence of this opinion.

must so far copy them that art criticism is embroiled in a perpetual controversy as to whether pictorial art must of necessity be representationalist, or need not be. What the painter makes is also a material thing. But the musician does not apparently imitate or copy any physical thing or things, nor does he make physical things.[1] Further he does not, or need not, use his hands to manipulate physical things when he is creating. Mozart saw his compositions as a whole and sometimes, apparently, in a flash. The business of transcribing them reduced itself, therefore, for him to something in the nature of a routine operation. Moreover Mozart does not leave us a physical thing as his 'work'. Admittedly physical things, waves, wires, horses' tails, entrails of sheep and cats and so forth, are necessary to enable his compositions to assume audible form. But it is not really necessary for those who are sufficiently gifted musically to *hear* his music, in order that they may appreciate it. There is significance too in the fact that music is traditionally regarded as the most impersonal of the arts, and, the greater the music, the more impersonal. Schnabel is reported to have said that he could find no difference between the music of Beethoven, Mozart and Schubert. A hard saying; yet Schnabel, presumably, knows what he is talking about. And what, I take it, he meant is that music can reach a level, the level of absolute form, of pure sound, at which the personality of the composer is completely transcended.

[1] For a possible qualification of this statement see my *Matter, Life and Value*, pp. 307-9.

II. Philosophy and Value

The meaning of such phrases as 'pure sound' or 'absolute form' is very difficult to express. But one of the things that is, I think, intended is that the vision of the artist has penetrated into a world in which a formal structure or rhythm is revealed, purged of the dross of matter with which it is normally clothed.[1] Plato's Form of Beauty, which is not the beauty of any individual thing, embodies the same conception. Now the hallmark of the greatest art is that it is super-personal in precisely this sense, the personality of the composer being lost in the degree to which he succeeds in achieving entrance into a world of pure, formal beauty. This super-personality is one of the distinctive features of Shakespeare's poetry. It is characteristic too of that 'last period' work of the greatest artists to whose peculiarities I have already referred. But it is realized more often in music than in any other art.

These may perhaps be some of the reasons why music has the greatest power over man's spirit of all the arts, a power which enables it to tear the soul of man like a cocoon from the chrysalis in which it is slowly maturing, and to endow it momentarily with a precocious puberty scarcely inferior in point of spiritual maturity to that of the mystic.[2] Music, in fact, is for some an enchantment revealing by its magic, to souls not yet prepared for it, a glory which only the original faculty of the genius, or

[1] See the last chapter, pages 229, 230, for an elaboration of this.
[2] E.g. its effect on Samuel Pepys:—'It ravished me, and, indeed, in a word, did wrap up my soul, so that it made me really sick, just as I have formerly been when in love with my wife.'

the long training and arduous discipline of the mystic or sage can reach unassisted.

(2) *Æsthetic Value in Philosophy.* Secondly, there is the curious fact, at which I have already glanced, that philosophical writing is capable not only of intellectual but of æsthetic evaluation. Prove a scientific theory to be false, and, save in the histories of science, it will never be heard of again. Pick holes in every page of the writings of a great philosopher, show his metaphysic as a whole to be untenable, and you prevent neither yourself nor anybody else from reading him again and again. A scientific theory, in fact, has no pretensions except to truth; expose them, and you dismiss the theory. For this reason, I should imagine, it must be a thankless task to plough through the works of a scientist whose general conclusions you know to be unsound, to see what you can pick up of value by the way.

But by philosophers the task is habitually and fruitfully performed. They know, for example, that Hume writes with heavenly detachment and exquisite lucidity, and that his works are packed with witty and entertaining comment. Hence, whatever they may think of his theory of the Association of Ideas, they read him because they wish to learn detachment, because they would like to be able to express philosophical ideas with the minimum of obscurity and fuss, and because they are amused and delighted with the catlike malice of the comments. Truth, in fact, is not all, for in addition to truth there is style; and behind style there is wisdom,

wisdom which is born of understanding and the ripe experience of life garnered by a powerful mind.

The Quality of Wisdom. Now wisdom finds its most appropriate form of expression in philosophy. It is wisdom when Aristotle informs us that we all tell a story with exaggerations in the belief that we are giving pleasure; Plato that it is the excesses of democracy that produce tyranny (we know it, alas, only too well in these later years, but who would have acclaimed this penetrating piece of political diagnosis at its true value before the war? But then the whole account of the decline of the State in Books VIII and IX of the *Republic* is a monument of political wisdom); or Russell that science does not change human desires and purposes, it only gives human beings a greater power of realizing their desires and furthering their purposes; or Whitehead that great ideas are like phantom oceans in the background of human consciousness 'beating upon the shores of human life in successive waves of specialization. A whole succession of such waves are as dreams slowly doing their work of sapping the base of some cliff of habit; but the seventh wave is a revolution— "And the nations echo round".' But apart from its wisdom, its fruitful treatment of particular topics, its incidental felicities of style and expression, a philosophy may have a further claim to make upon our attention, a claim which derives from its possession of value. We read the great philosophers not only for the possible truth of their systems, but for their ennobling, their

Plato as Artist

strictly elevating effect upon the mind. Some derive the benefit of this effect from Hegel, some from Spinoza, some from Kant; but it is, I think, in Plato that men have felt it most.

Plato as Artist. For my part, it is to Plato of all the philosophers that I most frequently turn, partly, I suspect, because the reading of Plato has become for me largely an æsthetic experience. Apart altogether from the question of whether his philosophy is strictly true, which is the question of whether the universe is really constituted as Plato supposes, it confers immediate enrichment upon the mind. To read Plato for the first time is to subject the mind to a process analogous to that whereby gloves are stretched by glove stretchers. As the experience proceeds, the reader can positively feel his mind being opened, pulled wider, made more capacious, so that at the end he is conscious of being a mental size larger than he was at the beginning. But to read Plato often is to experience an emotion more akin to that enjoyed when visiting a loved piece of country or hearing a familiar fugue. This effect, æsthetic rather than intellectual, is I think, largely the result of the nobility of Plato's themes, or, in the terminology I have adopted, of the aloofness from the physical world and of the corresponding nearness to the confines of the world of value of the objects of thought, the Platonic Forms, for example, upon which his mind plays. Plato more often than any other philosopher, 'breaks through'—he does it in the *Timæus*, in the *Phædo* and again at the end of the

II. Philosophy and Value

Republic—into the world of value, and, even when the veil remains undrawn, there is a sense of immanence in his work, as if it were at any moment about to be lifted. And Plato's writings, more than those of any other philosopher writer, are brushed by the wings of the beauty he has glimpsed, a beauty which shines the most brightly in his philosophically least coherent work. Plato seems at times like a man to whom there shoots down from the place where light is flashes and gleams which blind and dazzle him, so that, while the power of the vision is still upon him, he can tell of it only in confused and stammering words. Yet, when his mind has cleared, the memory has already faded.

Beauty of Mathematics. It is because of the affinity between the objects which they respectively study, that the resemblances between philosophy and mathematics are so numerous and so striking. Mathematics, unlike science but like philosophy, is susceptible of æsthetic valuation. Chains of reasoning are economical, solutions are elegant, the elimination of unnecessary hypotheses as pleasing as the elimination of unnecessary ornaments, while the demonstration that all mathematics follows necessarily from a small collection of fundamental laws is found æsthetically delightful by those who can grasp it. Those who love system, order and coherence, who are oppressed by the disorder and turmoil of the world, who are outraged by the haphazard and the unreasonable, to whom things which might just as well have been otherwise are an affront—

all such are gratified by the ordered necessity of the world of mathematics, in which whatever is purely general is presented in its entirety, stripped of the adventitious trappings which in the physical world distort and obscure it.

Plato, perhaps more than any other philosopher, was impressed by the æsthetically significant character of mathematics, and affirmed its objects to be among the most noble that the human mind could contemplate; so noble, indeed, that he regarded the contemplation of mathematical truth as a worthy occupation for the deity. There is in mathematics, he says, 'something which is *necessary* and cannot be set aside . . . and, if I mistake not, of divine necessity; for as to the human necessities of which the Many talk in this connection, nothing can be more ridiculous than such an application of the words. *Cleinas.* And what are these necessities of knowledge, Stranger, which are divine and not human? *Athenian.* Those things without some use or knowledge of which a man cannot become a God to the world, nor a spirit, nor yet a hero, nor able earnestly to think and care for man'.

To translate into the language I have been using, the objects of mathematics, like those of philosophy, stand on the furthest confines of the world of thought. For this reason they are at times tinged with the glow of the value that lies beyond, while those whose lives are spent in contemplating them are liable at any moment to 'break through' into that world.

II. Philosophy and Value

(3) *Philosophy in virtue of its Generality the Integrator of Personality.* A familiar way of putting the above conclusion is to emphasize the generality of the objects of mathematics and philosophy. The propositions of both, though they may be instanced by particular things and events, are independent of the physical phenomena which illustrate them. When we say that three and two make five, or that it is impossible for x both to be and not to be a so-and-so, the nature of the things summed by three and two and denoted by the symbol x is, as I have tried to show, irrelevant. I have already pointed out that it is quite unnecessary that there should be any *things* at all in order that the statements may be true. We are concerned, then, in philosophy, as in mathematics, with the *general* laws that underlie the behaviour of phenomena, but which are in no way dependent upon the existence of illustrating phenomena for their validity. Now the apprehension of generality requires a certain generalization of the apprehending faculties. Logic is pursued by reason, cruelty witnessed with emotion, secrets divined or intentions apprehended by intuition, duty performed from the promptings of the moral sense, music apprehended by the æsthetic sensibility; but, to the comprehension of that which is purely general, must go a synthesis of all the faculties; and, not least, of the specifically intellectual faculties.

It has been the persistent argument of previous chapters that each enlargement of human faculty, each acquisition of human skill, each extension of human sensibility or widening of human apprehension, is in the nature of a jump; that, whatever may be the case with nature, the human mind *omne facit per saltum.*

Value of Integration in Personality. The jump, I have argued, occurs after and only after continuous practice and exercise at the level *from* which it is made. Now these jumps are in the nature of integrations. They bring together into a new whole or unity faculties or aspects of human nature which had previously functioned separately. The best definition of a 'personality' known to me is a human being in whom all the different aspects of man's nature, mind and spirit, intellect and emotion, impulse and desire, tastes and sentiments are dovetailed into an harmonious whole, with the result that the whole force of the man is behind his every act, thought and wish. Such a man is a 'personality'.

At the other end of the scale there is dissociation of personality, where the degree of integration is so small that either the so-called person is only a bundle of scattered unitary faculties, or the faculties coalesce into not one but two or three grouped wholes, and we have cases such as that of Sally Beauchamp. Children are apt to be disintegrated, a child's life tending to be a procession of passions, impulses, desires, sadness, anger and gladness, which succeed one another, often with disconcerting abruptness. Integration, then, is a sign of maturity, of maturity that is at a given level. And, if my general formula is anywhere near the truth, it presages a jump to a new level.

II. Philosophy and Value

Vices of Departmentalism. Now the tastes and sentiments of the average man are—the observation is a platitude—highly departmentalized. He may acquire a religious sentiment, a family sentiment, a professional sentiment for his job, and a hobby sentiment, say for photography. Each of these sentiments recruits a complex system of intellectual abilities in its service, a system which remains distinct from the other systems, and develops in a watertight compartment from which the other interests of the whole are rigorously shut out. Thus a man can go through life a serious and professing Christian on Sundays, while cheerfully flouting every principle of the creed which he professes by the methods he adopts to earn a living during the rest of the week. There is, in fact, no connecting link between his religious and his professional department. Similarly, he will continue quite simply and sincerely to believe that the Commandments ought to be obeyed and that killing one's enemies is murder and, therefore, a crime, while cheerfully accepting the duty of killing other men whom he has never seen, whenever the State to which he happens to belong deems the mass slaughter of the citizens of another State desirable, and even in the name of patriotism taking a pride in the job. There is no bridge between his system of ethical beliefs and his patriotic sentiment.

Instances could be multiplied indefinitely; they suggest irresistibly that, so far as his beliefs and sentiments are concerned, the ordinary man is not one but many, not a star but a solar system.

Such departmentalized development is natural enough. It is none the less disastrous, civilization at the moment being in danger of destruction in consequence of an unprecedented development in man's mechanical skill and ability to exploit the forces of nature, with which his ethical sentiments and social wisdom have entirely failed to keep pace. The situation is familiar enough in mythology; the wicked fairy gives the innocent child attractive but dangerous toys, in the hope that he may compass his own destruction. In the world of grown-ups it is we who make the toys and then sell them to the wicked fairy.

Synthesis of Faculties effected by Philosophy. Now the advantage of an all-round as opposed to a specialized education is that it cultivates all the interests, and cultivates them together, resulting, if it is successful, not merely in systems but in a balanced system of systems, in which any aptitude, ability or sensibility, which has been cultivated in the interests of one branch of knowledge or one field of art, may be used impartially in the service of all.

Of such an education philosophy is the crown. First, logic or methodology is introduced to break down watertight compartments, by training the mind in the study of principles of reasoning which are seen to be both common to and invariable in all branches of knowledge. What logic does for the *principles* of reasoning in all the sciences, metaphysics does for their conclusions. It serves, as I pointed out in the seventh chap-

ter, as an intellectual clearing house to which the conclusions of the sciences are referred, and in which they
are pooled and sifted in order that their *general* implications may be gauged. Nor, as we have seen, is it only the
results of the special sciences that philosophy takes into
account, but data brought from other fields, from the
study of human beings in life and literature, from the
behaviour of human communities, from the intro-
spective examination of one's own experience in the
enjoyment of art and nature, from the analysis of the
content of moral obligation. Integrating various kinds
of experience, systems of knowledge and sets of conclusions, philosophy in accordance with our formula
prepares the mind for a jump beyond the conclusions.
Drawing into its net all the material garnered by the
exploring reason, philosophy prepares the mind for a
leap into the realms beyond reason.

(3) *Philosophical Intuition. The Intuitive Knowledge of
Persons.* This is perhaps the ground for the belief, in my
view the legitimate belief, that philosophy is an appropriate sphere for the activity of intuition. On the subject
of intuition, its scope, functions and limitations, I have
ventured to summarize in an earlier chapter[1] views expressed elsewhere. I am here concerned to emphasize
one point only which may be most conveniently
illustrated by an analogy.

Let us suppose that we were to endeavour to give a
really complete account of a human being. Inevitably,

[1] See Chapter I, pages 31, 32.

we should turn first to science. What, then, have the scientists to tell us? We should listen, first, to the physiologist's account in terms of tubes and pipes, nerves and bones and blood vessels. These, presumably, can be analysed into their chemical compounds, and there is therefore a chemist's account in terms of molecules and elements. These again can be analysed in terms of their atomic constituents, and there is, therefore, the physicist's account in terms of protons and electrons. Beginning at the other end of the scale, we should have to pay attention to the psychologist's account in terms of mental events, images, sensations and so forth, with special departmental accounts such as the behaviourist's in terms of language habits and conditioned reflexes, and the psycho-analyst's in terms of unconscious desire and promptings of the libido. From other points of view there is the economic man and the median man of the statistician; there is man from the standpoint of the biologist and man as he appears to the anthropologist. There is also the account of particular individual men to be found in the works of the great novelists. Each of these accounts could in theory be made accurate and complete—complete, that is to say, so far as it goes; yet each would be couched in different terms. To say that no one of these accounts conveys the whole truth about a man, but describes only some particular aspect of him which has been selected for special attention, would be to state a commonplace.

But more than this is implied in the current criticism of scientific method as concerned with abstractions. It is implied that, if all the different accounts, the physiological, the chemical, the physical, the psychological, the behaviouristic, the psycho-analytic, the economic, the statistical, the biological, the anthropological and the novelist's, were collated, supplemented by other accurate and complete but partial accounts and worked up into a comprehensive survey, they would still fail to constitute *the* truth about a man. And they would fail to do this, not because some particular piece of information had been left out, or some particular point of view forgotten—for, it would be urged, no matter how complete the collection of scientific accounts might be, *the* truth would still elude them—but because they would remain only a set of separate accounts of different parts or aspects, and a man is more than the different parts or aspects which are ingredients of him. True knowledge of a man is not, in other words, the sum total of the complete and accurate accounts of all his different aspects, even if those accounts could be made exhaustive. True knowledge is, or at least includes, knowledge of the man as a whole. To know a man as a whole is to know him as a personality, for a personality is the whole which, while it integrates all the parts and so includes them within itself, is nevertheless something over and above their sum.

Now to know a man as a personality is to know him in a manner of which science takes no cognizance. Also it is to know him in a way which is not rational, in the sense that no account can be given of it. The conclusion which has been so often suggested in these pages again emerges. When reason has done her utmost, the mind may make a leap to the exercise of a new activity beyond reason.

(4) *Where Philosophy Transcends Reason.* It is this activity which in philosophy we know as intuition, in art as æsthetic sensibility, in ethics as moral insight. It is an activity of integration, but it operates not so much to achieve an integration at the old level, as to effect the advance to a new one when the integration at the old has already been achieved. The activities of the human mind in philosophy are very numerous; philosophy in fact challenges more of our faculties, appeals to more sides of our nature than any other form of intellectual pursuit, because, perhaps, in the last resort it is more than an intellectual pursuit.

Of these manifold activities the bulk are in the strict sense rational; they are the activities of reason. There is, for example, the assessment of the empirical facts collected by science, the reading of our own experience, the acquaintance with the work of other philosophers, the interpretation of that work in the light of the scientist's facts and the report of our experience, the gradual formation of a set of provisional conclusions with regard to the resultant data viewed as a whole. Secondly, and perhaps only in the greatest philosophers, there is to be found an activity of insight or vision which, passing beyond the data collected, realizes a level of apprehension at which a new order of the universe is glimpsed, an order to which the mystic has occasional, the artist still more intermittent access, but which may one day become the natural field for the contemplation of all human consciousness, as the realm of thought-objects is the natural field of its awareness to-day. It is because of their occasional 'breaks through' into this field that intuition is attributed to the great philosophers, and is commonly regarded as a legitimate part of the philosophic activity.

The great thinker, expressing in allegory or myth that which outruns the limit of rational presentation, is one of the best-accredited, if not one of the most familiar figures on the philosophical scene, and even the most unintelligible passages of Plato, Plotinus or Samkara are recognized as the products of great minds, greatly engaged.

My conclusion is, then, that there is a moment in the philosopher's vision when logical truth is transcended and there is a direct intuitive vision of that which lies beyond, a territory which is, I would suggest, not fundamentally different from that approached by the mystic and the artist.

The Philosopher as a 'Character'. It is, perhaps, partly for this reason that the philosopher is traditionally regarded as a certain sort of man. From among the various types of intellectuals, the historians, the scientists, the classical scholars, the economists, the novelists, even the mathematicians, it is pre-eminently the philosopher who is picked out as a man apart, a poor bemused fellow unable to catch trains, to answer letters, to cross the road, or to perform the simplest offices of daily life. He is in fact *par excellence* the type of the absent-minded man. He is also a man whom Plato represents as sheltering behind a wall from a storm, intending, I imagine, to indicate that the philosopher is 'on the defensive' against life.

The common conception is, of course, a caricature. Nevertheless there would not be so much smoke without a little flame, and there can, I think, be no reasonable doubt that because of the nature of their preoccupations philosophers have upon the whole—and with notable exceptions such as Socrates or John Stuart Mill—been noticeably indifferent to the affairs of this world. And their minds are, I suggest, 'absent' for the reason that they are normally occupied with the consideration of matters that belong not merely to the world of thought but lie, if I may revert to my metaphor, on its furthest horizon. In proportion as the objects of his attention are the farther removed, the greater is the philosopher's effort in withdrawing his mind and concentrating it upon the world of every day. It is greater for example than is the effort of the historian or the scientist.

If we conceive the mystic as one who, in Plato's famous simile, has ventured from the cave into the world outside, then, while we must in the last resort deny to the philosopher the privilege of sharing in the mystic's sunlight, we may, I would suggest, at least concede to him a place nearer to the mouth of the cave than that of any of his fellow workers in the world of thought. He works like them in the darkness, but it is a darkness which is from time to time irradiated by chance beams of the sunlight that shoot down from above. It is to this double fact, that the objects of his attention are situated on the far horizon of the world of thought, and that the philosopher himself is, in Plato's phraseology, while still a denizen of the cave, yet stationed on the threshold of the world beyond it, that most of the peculiar characteristics of philosophy are, I would suggest, due.

Mystical Element in Philosophy. Like literature or art, philosophy is, as we have seen, entitled—nay more, it demands—to be judged by æsthetic criteria. The writing of philosophy is eloquent, inspired or lucid, as its themes are noble, profound or ingenious. It is not without significance that famous passages from Bacon, from Bradley, or from Hume find their way into anthologies of English prose. Some of these passages are strangely moving; they are even exciting. This excitement which pervades the great passages of philosophy may, I am suggesting, like the excitement of the mystics or of great art, be a reflection of some character of the world of value to which the philosophic vision has penetrated, as the books in a library opening to the west catch the reflected glow of the setting sun. Into philosophy written in the grand manner there creeps a certain sense of imminence. At any one moment, one feels, the writer may 'break through' into a different world, different and more exciting. Meanwhile, so near is that world, that it is impossible not to realize its agitating proximity. And, like the great musicians, sometimes the philosophers do in fact 'break through'. It is as if reason, dwelling always among objects neighbouring upon Value and stretched to the uttermost by the arduous nature of its subject matter, gives way on occasion under the strain, and permits the mind to pass temporarily into a realm beyond reason. Hence the mystical passages in the works of the great philosophers; the myths in which they seek to embody meanings incapable of rational statement; the inspired dogmatisms which, striking us with a feeling of utter rightness and conveying an air of complete certitude, seem to be less the products of the intellect than of a faculty akin to the vision of the mystic and the seer. Hence, too, the difficulty, to which I have already referred, of drawing the line between metaphysics and moonshine and distinguishing the utterance of the profoundest cosmic truths from the pretentious pontificatings of my philosophic stockbrokers.

And hence, finally, the paradox that it is not enough to ask of a philosophy that it should be true; often, indeed, its truth would seem to be the least important thing about it. If it elevates and ennobles the mind, if it so strains and stretches the reason that it snaps like a taut thread to give way to a faculty more rare and penetrating; if it brings the philosopher to the threshold of the world of value, and if, while doing all this for those who create it, it is not without its humbler effects upon those who read it merely, making them tolerant in opinion, tentative in conclusion, understanding in judgment, impartial in decision, serene in mind and arming them against the slights and piques of this world in proportion as it gives them the view of another; if it does any part of these things, all of which it has it in its power to do, then philosophy may be accounted not only an escape, one of the most certain, from the uncertainties and transiencies of the world of becoming, but a window—less clear than art or religion, but a window nevertheless—through which the consciousness of man attains a vision of the world of being.

Epilogue

★

Intrusion of the Topical. Here, I suppose, this book should appropriately end. It is a book concerned in the main with generalities, with what the nineteenth century called the eternal verities, and I have endeavoured, especially in these later chapters, to exclude from it all matters relative to locality of time and space. It is not in intention a topical book, and in the carrying out of its intention it has remained as little topical as the stresses and pressures of the times would permit. And yet, in spite of all I could do to exclude them, the here and the now have always been present, perpetually pressing for acknowledgment and recognition. Having successfully withheld acknowledgment during the last three chapters, I now feel myself constrained by their claims to a quite peculiar relevance to my concluding theme, to admit them and see what they have to say for themselves. They have two comments to make, and they promise that both shall be brief.

As I write, the air is full of preparations for war and rumours of war. The counter-revolution has taken place in Germany, and those hardly won goods of civilized man, free thought, free speech, a free press and freedom for the individual to live his life as seems best to him have disappeared from large areas of the Continent. Many prophesy the end of our civilization owing to man's inability to control the powers with which science has endowed him.

The contemporary situation bears in two ways upon the theme with which I have been engaged, and enables me to offer two specifically topical contributions to the defence of philosophy which I have tried to draw up.

The Failure to Connect. I have stressed the function of philosophy as a synthesizer. It acts, I have suggested, as a clearing house of knowledge, breaking down watertight compartments and introducing connections between the different departments of human thought and activity. Philosophy in a word helps men to connect. Now it might be plausibly urged that failure to connect is one of the major disabilities of modern man, a disability which has become a danger to our civilization.

As I write, human beings contemplate the increasing preparations for their own destruction not with fear but calmly, even rapturously. Crowds flock to watch army aeroplanes skirmishing in the skies. A thousand screens show bombs dropping, guns firing, torpedoes being launched, poison gas diffused, to audiences who watch them with a passionate interest. Nobody protests; nobody is driven by the most elementary law of self-preservation to demand that these preparations should be stopped. Why not? Because of a failure to connect. It never occurs to these applauding crowds that these instruments of destruction, upon whose preparation they are prepared to lavish immense wealth and whose efficiency gives them the most complacent satisfaction, may be, probably will be used against themselves. Not, perhaps, those particular guns or planes which they are watching at Aldershot or at Hendon, but guns and planes exactly like them which are being prepared and perfected a few thousand miles away; not but what the very weapons which they admire are sometimes sold to those who become their enemies, and use them for the destruction of the watchers. And to the directors of armament firms who make these things and are prepared to sell them to all comers, to the clergy and members of Parliament, the judges and doctors and dons and gentlefolk who derive incomes from the business of their manufacture, it never seems to occur that their money is being used to trade in death, and that the potential source of their wealth is the shattered bodies, the scorched skins, the sightless eyes, the burst lungs of those whom the guns have dismembered, burnt, blinded and asphyxiated. They do not realize, or seem not to, that their profits are derived from the agony of human beings, and that these human beings may be themselves.

And those newspaper proprietors in all countries who are also the directors of armament firms—do not the profits on a single battleship amount to more than the few millions required to purchase a newspaper, lock, stock and barrel?—whose papers are continually fomenting men's fears and inflaming their pride, they and their editors and their leader writers, while they are personally kindly men, who do not wish anyone to be hurt and think in terms of sales and advertisements rather than of policies and programmes, never appear to conceive that by their persistent advocacy of a militant nationalism, their persistent crabbing of such poor machinery of peace as a distracted world has managed to contrive, they may be conniving at their own destruction. And the patriotic teachers, the professors of military history, the lecturers on war strategy, remote donnish men who certainly do not delight in the mass slaughter of their fellows, never seem to relate the duty to country they so eloquently prescribe, or the battles whose strategy they so ably expound to dismembered and disembowelled human bodies.

People, the fact is alas all too clear, have not been trained to remark the correlations of things. They do not perceive connections. Now one of the main functions of philosophy is, as we have seen, the function of correlation. It breaks down watertight compartments and summons all knowledge and experience to judgment at the same bar. A little philosophy will assist men to connect and, in helping connection, will help also the civilization that is so dangerously menaced by its lack.

Philosophy as an Antidote. Secondly, it is, I believe, a fact that many of those who are normally engaged in research or creative work find it difficult to-day to pursue their ordinary avocations. Nor are their difficulties merely economic. Over many of the sensitive-minded

Philosophy as an Antidote

men and women of this generation hangs the menace of a great fear; the fear of the destruction by war of such civilization as we have achieved. Because of it their minds are unable to escape from the preoccupations of the political scene. Even if their preoccupation cannot prevent or even delay for the fraction of a second the catastrophe, they cannot withdraw their fascinated gaze from the spectacle of its slow approach. Physics and psycho-analysis, literature and art, the novel of the year, the latest experiment in poetry, So-and-so's 'show' of paintings, such and such a performance of a symphony, these, which used to be the main staples of conversation in circles which in the long run form the taste and set the standards of the community, are now neglected for discussions of rearmament and dictatorship.

And, inevitably, first-rate literary and artistic production falters or ceases altogether. How can a man think, let alone dream, when the hills and valleys are filled with the echoes of marching feet? How can he command the serenity to conceive or the patience to create beautiful things, when he contemplates the prospect of those whom he loves being slowly asphyxiated by gas and the fruits of his effort being scattered with the ashes of the civilizations that gave it birth? The creative artist demands a quiet background, if he is to produce his best work; he also requires an audience whose release from the more primitive preoccupations of the soldier, the savage and the gangster enables them to turn their attention to the products of the spirit. He demands in fact a civilized environment, alert, interested, reasonably secure. Under the stresses and fears of our time such an environment is fast vanishing from the Europe of to-day, and, as a result, the interest of civilized people in the art and literature of their times shows a corresponding decline. In some of the preceding pages I have noted this decline, contrasting a civilization which produced as its characteristic work Chartres Cathedral with the standardized products and creation-saving pursuits of our own, and dwelling upon the revolt against reason and the modern cult of the primitive. These things are, I suggest, the appropriate manifestations of a threatened civilization sensing and fearing its end.

But, while men can no longer create, while they find it hard even to appreciate with serene minds, they can still pursue philosophy. Ever since Socrates philosophized on the threshold of death, philosophy has solaced men in times of misfortune. In philosophy men who are agitated can find peace, men who are wretched resignation, men who are afraid courage. The charge against philosophy that it makes us absent-minded is not wholly to be deplored. For to withdraw the mind from the things of this world is not in itself a good or an evil. It is an evil, if the things from which we are withdrawn are mainly good, a good if they are mainly evil.

Index

★

Adler 35, 165
Alexander, Professor 17, 19
Alexander the Great 194
Anaximander 158
Aristotle 38, 156, 176, 183, 194, 254

Bach 60, 63, 77, 80, 83, 85, 90, 100, 106-7, 197, 236
Bacon 268
B.B.C. 106
Beauchamp, Sally 259
Beethoven 83-5, 89, 90, 236-237, 251
Bell, Clive 95, 97
Bennett, Arnold 16
Bentham 76
Berkeley 134
Blake 86
Botticelli 90-1
Bradley 141, 172, 268
Breton, M. 144
Browning 91
Bunyan 86
Butler, Bishop 38, 183, 185, 187

Butler, Samuel 141
Byrd 105

Casanova 88
Chesterton 17, 150
Chopin 91
Christian Science 47-57
Cobbett 88, 101

Dali, Salvador 144
Descartes 115-6, 124, 152, 194
Dickens, 11, 231
Dolmetsch family, the 105

Eddington 15, 17, 19, 135
Eddy, Mrs. 30, 47-8, 52-4, 56
Einstein 15, 131-2
Ellis, Havelock 134
Emerson 86
Epstein 143

Faulkner 148
Forster 64
Freud 35, 165

277

Index

Galileo 152
Garbo, Greta 91
Gaskell, Mrs. 80
Goering 88
Guyon, Mme. 145

Handel 63
Hardy, Thomas 16, 25, 92
Hegel 15, 255
Hemingway 79, 148
Henley 87
Hitler, Adolf 88
Houghton, Claude 148-9
Hume 134, 194, 253, 268
Huxley, Aldous (*passim*) 26-27, 35, 72-88, 103, 109-11, 113-38, 147, 149-52, 163, 167-8, 170, 175-8, 180, 188-9, 191, 193-5, 197, 199, 200
Hylton, Jack 90

Inge 17, 19

Jack the Ripper 77
Jeans 15, 17
Jenkins 105
Joyce 64
Jung 35, 165

Kant 134, 152, 193, 255
Keats 90
Kensit, J. A. 86

Lawes 105
Lawrence, D. H. 35, 142-7, 149, 167-8, 197-200
Leavis, F. R. & Q. D. 63-4
Locke 105, 134

Low 81

Mantegna 79
McDougall 165
Mendelssohn 89
Meredith 90, 92
Michelangelo 77, 90-1
Mill, James 76
Mill, J. S. 75-6, 78, 147, 153, 267
Mozart 60, 77, 231, 251

Nerval 144
Newton 152

Pascal 74, 79, 113, 115-6, 120, 132, 176
Pater 92
Patmore 92
Pepys, Samuel 252 *note*
Planck 15, 107
Plato 15, 94-6, 98, 101, 147, 177, 184, 194, 232-4, 237, 246, 252, 254-6, 266-7
Plotinus 266
Puccini 91
Purcell 105
Pythagoreans, the 162

Quiller-Couch 232

Richards, I. A. 154, 167, 170
Rossetti, D. G. 91
Ruskin 87, 91
Russell, Bertrand 17, 248, 254

St. John of the Cross 145
Samkara 266

278

Index

'Sapper' 91
Scarlatti 63
Schnabel 90, 251
Schopenhauer 37-8
Schubert 63, 84, 251
Shakespeare 90, 100, 235, 237, 252
Shaw, G. B. 16-7, 19, 41, 64, 86, 147, 237
Socrates 14, 33, 76, 151, 194, 203, 267
Spencer, Herbert 153
Spinoza 14, 194, 255
Stevenson, R. L. 87, 91
Stout 165
Stoics, the 54
Stravinsky 143
Sweden, Queen of 152, 194
Swift 86

Tauler 146

Thales 15, 157-8
Thomson, James (B.V.) 92
Thompson, Francis 91-2
Torquemada 77, 88
Turner, W. J. 11 *note*

Vaihinger 134
Vermeer 97

Wagner 106
Wallace, Edgar 90
Watson 165
Wells, H. G. 17, 64
Whitehead 254
Wilde 92
Wood, Sir Henry 106
Woodworth 165
Woolf, Virginia 64
Wordsworth 90
Wren 91